A PIECE OF CLOTH

A PIECE OF CLOTH

The Turin Shroud Investigated

by

Rodney Hoare

THE AQUARIAN PRESS
Wellingborough, Northamptonshire

First published 1984

BT
587
.S4
H58
1984

British Library Cataloguing in Publication Data

Hoare, Rodney
   A Piece of Cloth.
   1. Holy Shroud
   I. Title
   232.9'66   BT587.S4

   ISBN 0-85030-419-9

The Aquarian Press is part of the
Thorsons Publishing Group

Printed in Great Britain by
Butler & Tanner Ltd, Frome and London

CONTENTS

INTRODUCTION

I can clearly remember when I first heard about the piece of cloth known as the Turin Shroud. In 1955 the magazine *Picture Post* published an article on it written by Group Captain Leonard Cheshire, and the impressive, uncanny images of the front and back of a man's body recorded on the cloth immediately intrigued me. They were haunting in their realism and majesty. I would have expected them to have been painted for some religious purpose, but apparently there were no signs of paint on the cloth, and the reversed images on the negative were even more remarkable than on the positive. How could any painter achieve that effect even now, let alone centuries ago? It made no sense.

'I love to lose myself in a mystery, to pursue my Reason to *O altitudo!*' wrote Sir Thomas Browne[1] in about 1635. Who does not? First find a suitable mystery. This particular one fascinated me far more than any other I have encountered. It suited me admirably as a physicist and photographer, and I felt that if the cloth were genuine, its message would be supremely important.

In 1972 I moved to Nottingham, and had more time to 'lose myself in a mystery'. Group Captain Cheshire's address was listed in *Who's Who,* so I wrote to him asking how I could obtain large positive and negative photographs of the

Shroud. He replied most kindly and told me the source, and soon I was able to study them in detail.

The strange feeling connected with an obsession is that everyone else does not share it. Once addicted, one can so easily become a bore. My family made me aware of the danger, in the nicest possible way, helping me to acquire a sense of proportion and keep my friends. After a time my attitude changed, so that I was happily surprised when a person showed considerable interest, which is the way it ought to be.

Soon after this I had to give a lecture to a small, informal group of students at Nottingham College of Education, where I was a lecturer, and I decided to tell them about the piece of cloth and what could be deduced from the stains. I called it, rather dramatically, 'The Oldest Photograph in the World'. They were fascinated, and subsequently I was asked to address an entire year group, perhaps three hundred students, on the subject. You cannot simply chat to an audience that size: you must know your subject. Thorough preparation was necessary, and I did not have enough material for a lecture.

Inspiration came. The stains showed a crucified man, and so were evidence of a terrible crime. The people to consult would be the forensic scientists. I rang the local police, explaining I needed to have expert advice before making accusations concerning a crime; fortunately they treated it seriously and put me in touch with the East Midlands forensic science laboratory in Nottingham. I was lucky on two counts; firstly, because I had a renowned group of forensic scientists locally; and secondly, because my unorthodox approach worked and I was allowed to consult them.

Across the Atlantic an author with a similar problem, Robert K. Wilcox, tried to enlist the FBI's help. His approach was the correct one; he sent them photographs of the stains on the Shroud and asked them to attempt an analysis of the cause of death. The FBI reply was:

> Our normal policy requires that the FBI laboratory conduct examinations of evidence in criminal cases for all duly constituted law enforcement agencies. Although exceptions to

this policy are possible, it has been found that examinations of the type you requested are not productive. Examination of the original material would be a more appropriate procedure; however, since such material is in custody of another country, it is not within the province of this Bureau to conduct such examinations.[2]

No doubt the Nottingham experts should have returned me a similar reply. However, as I have related in another book,[3] they did see me and were extremely helpful.

Luck had a large part to play in all this. Not only were friends at the College of Education, and later Trent Polytechnic when the College was absorbed into it, knowledgeable and interested, but I had a great deal of help from Nottingham University Chemistry Department, under Professor Turner, and the Theology Department, under Professor Heywood-Thomas. Had I lived somewhere comparatively isolated, like Chaddesley Corbett or Stoke-by-Nayland, or even in a metropolis with less helpful experts around, it would have been a different story.

That was an exciting time. The suggestions made by the forensic scientists started me off on a chain of ideas, which led to the consultations necessary for the next steps forward. Quite a number of suggestions came from the audiences at my lectures. By 1977 I had enough material for a book, and in 1978 *The Testimony of the Shroud* was published.

It may be legitimately asked why I have written another book on the Shroud. Is there any more to say?

There is a great deal to say. Later in 1978 was held the first exhibition of the Shroud since 1933. When the last of the crowds had seen it, the cloth was offered for a whole week to teams of American and Italian scientists to examine, using any methods they liked that did not destroy or damage any material. All those results have since been published. Also, working from the photographs, I myself have done more practical work on the stains since 1978 than I had done before. But the main reason another book is required is because the whole approach needed revising.

The problem is this. The piece of cloth is regarded by many as having religious significance. The custodians are the

Roman Catholic Church, and the sanction of the Archbishop of Turin has been necessary before anyone has been allowed access to it. There is a good side to this; but on the other hand, much of the work on the Shroud has been done by committed Christians. Unfortunately, the instant religion enters the study there is no possibility of objectivity.

Faith forbids impartiality; it steers deductions in the direction of its own beliefs, or else the evidence is disregarded or vilified. A man of faith who wishes to be objective must be prepared to lose that faith. He is like a sailor shipwrecked on a tropical island. To find out if there is anything better over the horizon he must be willing to leave the safety of his island, knowing he can return to it. Yet unless he ventures on the journey, he cannot be completely happy. He is suppressing a doubt.

The Shroud is a material object, and as such can be investigated scientifically. Only by examining the evidence, and objectively deciding what conclusions can be drawn, can the message of the cloth be deciphered.

Unfortunately, you have almost certainly heard of the Turin Shroud already. You may have already formed your opinions on it, based on what you have heard or read. If so, try, please, to empty out those ideas. This book is written for an open mind. I have tried to keep religion out of the scientific analysis of the cloth. It is the story of the mystery I have followed, and I would like you also to 'pursue my Reason' objectively and see if you come to the same '*O altitudo!*'

References

1. *Religio Medici,* part 1,9. '*O altitudo!*' was probably a quotation from the Vulgate version of Romans 11,33: 'O depth of wealth, wisdom and knowledge in God!'
2. Wilcox, R. K., *Shroud,* Corgi, 1978, pp. 135-6.
3. Hoare, R. P., *The Testimony of the Shroud,* Quartet, 1978, pp. 47-55.

Part One

THE CLOTH

One

THE PIECE OF CLOTH

On 19 March 1983, the former King Umberto II of Italy died in Geneva. In his will he left a piece of cloth, which had belonged to his family for more than 430 years, to the Vatican.

Since 1578 that piece of cloth has been in Turin almost the whole time. It is known as the Turin Shroud. Its ownership was not seriously disputed from then until 1946, when King Umberto II was exiled after a plebiscite and the republic was inaugurated in Italy. The Shroud remained in Turin, under the guardianship of the Archbishop. Since the authorities of the state assumed ownership of other property of the king, including the palace in whose chapel the piece of cloth is stored, they might have claimed ownership of this as well. However, the Italian courts decided the cloth still belonged to ex-King Umberto,[1] so presumably it was his to give to the Vatican. Presumably, but not certainly.

On 18 October 1983, ex-King Umberto's executors formally met representatives of the Holy See to hand over the title to the Shroud. The media in Italy gave this meeting wide coverage, and no objection was raised by the state. Since then it has been assumed that the ownership of the cloth by the Pope and his successors is assured.

Those granted permission to examine it and lent the

The Cathedral in Turin. The far cupola is over the Chapel in which the Shroud is kept.

The Chapel. The grilles guarding the Shroud can be seen behind the candles.

required keys must climb steps near the main altar in the cathedral and enter the ornate Baroque chapel once used for private worship by the dukes of Savoy. It is rather sombre, for not much light comes from the cupola above, and much of the marble is black. Towering in the centre is the large, tall edifice containing the cloth.

From the floor its outer container can be seen some way up through iron grilles, and it is necessary to climb on the lower altar to reach it. The grilles have to be unlocked and the painted wooden outer container removed. Within this is an iron chest wrapped in asbestos, and inside this again is a four-foot long wooden casket with silver ornamentation.[2] In it is a red roll of material round a velvet staff. The red silk is the backing, and only on unwrapping it can the piece of cloth itself by found.

As the ivory-coloured material is revealed, the first surprise, perhaps, is its size. It is more than fourteen feet long, which means it is longer than the main room in most people's houses. It is also over three and a half feet wide. The material is linen. It feels very soft and pliable, and in weight

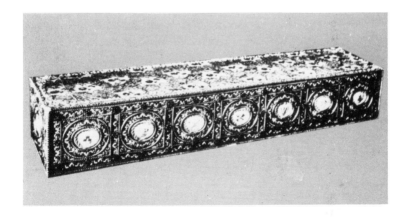

The chest that holds the Shroud.

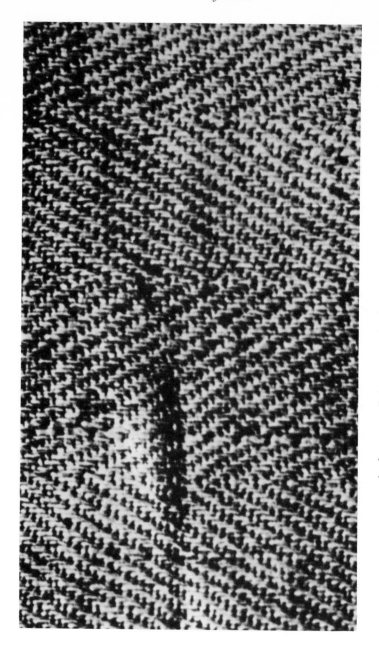

A close-up of the material of the Shroud.

somewhat heavier than shirt cloth.[3] The weave is tight, with the diagonals of a three-to-one twill weave visible, the same pattern used these days for cotton overalls and jeans.[4] What this means is that the weft, which is the thread manipulated by the weaver, is passed alternatively over three and under one of the warp threads, the ones that run the length of the cloth attached to the loom. This pattern is very good for resisting creasing and curling, and also wears very well. The cloth itself is in excellent condition, and the yarn used is remarkably regular. It is pure linen, except for odd traces of cotton on both the warp and weft threads.[5]

Unfortunately details such as these neither date the cloth nor locate its place of manufacture with any precision. Linen lasts centuries in very good condition. Moth grubs need materials containing keratin to feed on, like wool and feathers, and other insects find the flax fibres too hard.[6] Linens woven about 6000 years ago can be seen in Egyptian museums,[7] and quite a number of museums in Britain have linen cloths that are thousands of years old.

Nor is the regularity of the yarn indicative of recent manufacture. This depends on the knowledge and skill of the spinner as much as anything. The processes take time as well as care, two expensive commodities these days, so that the hand-spinners of ancient flax yarns at least matched the regularity of yarn used now.[8]

The three-to-one twill weave should be indicative of the cloth's age, but opinion varies on this point. One author claims that some of the cloths found in the tombs of King Sethos I (c. 1300 BC), Ramses III (1200 BC) and Queen Makeri (1100 BC) are woven in the same three-to-one twill pattern.[9] Another reports that three-to-one twill designs in linen are still preserved in the East from a time well before Christ.[10] Yet another denies all this and is unable to find any pre-medieval equivalent to the Turin Shroud.[11] Part of the problem may be the profusion of Egyptian linen cloths of plain weave, preserved by the funeral rites of the Egyptians and the dry atmosphere in the tombs. There is no doubt that the technology for producing a three-to-one twill in linen existed very early on: it is simply that no examples have been preserved. Woollen textiles have been found in Northern

Europe with such weaves dating from the Late Bronze Age, or about 4000 years ago.[12]

A more significant feature is the presence of odd fibres of cotton, identified as *Gossypium Herbaceum,* which, like flax, grows in the Middle East. The importance of this is not simply the presence of the cotton, but the absence of any woollen fibres. Every European loom would have been used mainly for wool, and woollen fibres would have been present in considerable numbers. The cloth, therefore, was not of European origin.

Another line of evidence corroborates this. Plants scatter pollen in abundance, for the chance of any one air-borne spore meeting with the appropriate female part of a plant of the same species is very small. The air contains masses of spores in summer, as all hay-fever sufferers know, and they settle everywhere. Microbes then attack them, and after a time only the pollen walls remain. However, these are characteristic of the species, and they can be used by forensic scientists to determine where items of clothing have been, for instance.

A Swiss criminologist, Dr Max Frei, pressed some sticky tape on parts of the Shroud in 1969, and examined the pollen that came off. He found that it was from forty-nine different plants, thirty-three of which grow only in Palestine, Anatolia and the area round Istanbul. [13]

Although precise conclusions regarding the time and place of manufacture cannot be drawn from these facts, some approximate ones can. The cloth was woven on a hand-loom somewhere in the Middle East, probably not Egypt, perhaps Syria or Palestine. The date is difficult to judge. One expert has narrowed it down to the first to third centuries AD,[14] but this is probably too specific on the evidence. It could be some time on either side of that range.

Scientists do have a tool at their disposal that could date the cloth fairly exactly if permission were granted for them to use it. This is the carbon dating process. There is a certain proportion of radio-active carbon to normal carbon in the atmosphere. When plants and animals are alive, an exchange of molecules continually takes place that ensures the proportion in their bodies is the same as that of the air around them. When they die this exchange stops. The radioactive carbon decays at a fixed rate, so by determining the proportion left in any object made from organic matter, it is possible to tell when the original plant or animal from which it was formed died.

For years requests for this experiment to be carried out were refused because a considerable amount of cloth would have had to be destroyed. But methods have improved dramatically. No more than a milligram would be required for modern equipment. That would enable an estimate to within an accuracy of about 150 years in 2000, which would be of the greatest importance in determining further research on the cloth. At the moment there is a broad division of opinion among scientists. Some feel certain the cloth was painted in the fourteenth century, while others claim the image was formed by natural means in the first, so that the dispute between them could be easily settled. Nor would it mean damaging the cloth. An area of about one square centimetre would be ample, and more than enough has already been cut off the Shroud. Not only this but it is estimated that behind the patches covering places damaged by fire lies approximately 400 square centimetres, and the Shroud would be safer with such charred material removed. That would be enough for many hundreds of tests.[15] The refusal of the Roman Catholic custodians to grant permission is difficult to understand.

While the exact time and place of manufacture is uncertain, there can be no doubt that the Shroud is a beautifully made length of cloth, and probably cost a very great deal. This has prompted the suggestion that it was intended as apparel rather than a shroud.[16] There is a lot of sense to this. A shroud would probably have been made from the simplest weave, which is why the funeral cloths that have been preserved from early times are nearly all plain. Garments do not survive so frequently. Incidentally, it is worth noting that this material would have been allowed under the Mosaic Law, for in the Mishna flax may have impurities of cotton. Flax and wool were strictly forbidden, however; as it says in Leviticus (19: 19), 'Ye shall keep my statutes. Thou shalt not . . . neither shall a garment mingled of linen and woollen come upon thee.'

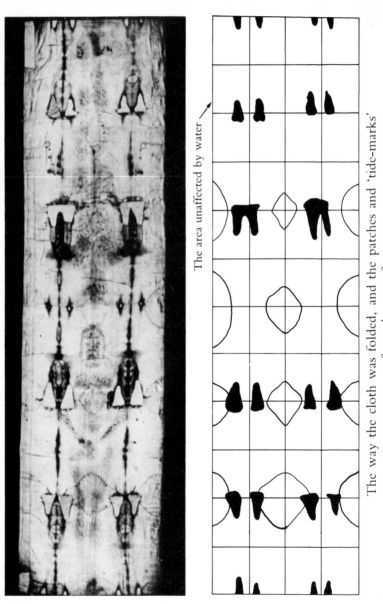

The area unaffected by water →

The way the cloth was folded, and the patches and 'tide-marks' from the 1532 fire.

So much for the material itself. On it, marks can be seen, faint and of a pale sepia colour, standing out from the ivory background.

The most obvious ones are the result of fire damage. While the cloth was kept in the sacristy of the Sainte Chappelle in Chambery, France, the building caught fire on the night of 4 December 1532. Within a short time the whole chapel was in flames. Two laymen and two Franciscan priests ran in at great risk, broke into the reliquary, grabbed the silver casket containing the cloth and rushed out with it. They must have been terribly burnt, for the casket was so hot that some of the silver melted, falling on to a corner of the folded cloth inside.[17]

The scars reveal how it was folded then – twice along the length, cutting its width into four, and then again so that it was only one twelfth the original length. The side of the casket that was hottest scorched the entire length one quarter from each long edge, the centre and long edges being unaffected as they were on the cool side. Where the molten silver fell, near a bunched corner, small areas of the cloth were burnt right through. The men poured on water to stop the charring.

The results of that night's ordeal can be seen on the cloth in several places. The charred lines running the length have already been mentioned. At intervals along those lines can be seen the patches stitched on by Poor Clare nuns in 1534 to cover the most damaged areas. The other signs are the 'tide marks', which show where the water reached.

The most interesting and important marks on the cloth are along the middle, between the scorches and patches. It is astonishing that these particular stains were not damaged by the fire, and one eyewitness at least, Pingone, a Baron of Savoy, has described his amazement, when the damaged Shroud was unfolded after the fire, in finding that the crucial stains, which give the cloth its importance, had scarcely suffered at all.[18]

With the naked eye these particular stains can only barely be seen. In 1978 the Shroud was on public exhibition in the Cathedral, held in a giant frame above and behind the main altar. Filing past it, ten or twelve feet away, the main impression of visitors was how little could be perceived. The brightness of the spotlights on it may have been partly responsible. The crucial stains were caused by, or represent, the front and back of a naked man's body, the two heads towards the centre of the cloth. Even to those who knew what they were looking for, only the few marks of blood, the dim shape of the head, the underneath of the soles, the hands, and one or two other vague marks could be seen. Those who have been privileged to see the cloth close to have also been astonished by how pale and subtle the image appears.[19] And the closer the eye moves to the cloth the more mysteriously the image dissolves.

The size of the image is part of the problem, for the stains change in intensity very gradually, so that there is insufficient contrast in a small area for the eye to perceive when close to the cloth.

Those who are familiar with photographs of the cloth are particularly surprised by the dimness of the image when they first see the Shroud. They will have seen black-and-white pictures of quite remarkable detail. In them the man stands out from the background quite clearly, and minute details of his features, form and wounds can be studied. This improvement is only to a small extent because the contrast is on a smaller scale so the eye can see it. It is principally because of the characteristics of film. From the first photographs taken in 1898, the sepia has been recorded by film as much darker than the background, so the contrast has been stepped up naturally. When the main black-and-white photographs used in research from 1931 onwards were taken by Giuseppe Enrie, orthochromatic film was used, and older readers will remember how that film used to leave blue skies white while it darkened red so drastically that the lips in a portrait came out black. It is not just with black-and-white film that the contrast is stepped up, for the same seems to happen with colour emulsions.

What is surprising is the clarity with which the marks of the man's body are shown in old paintings and engravings of the Shroud, and described in documents. The Poor Clares who repaired the cloth after the fire left a remarkably detailed description, which, judging from the accounts of modern observers, would be difficult to obtain by eye from the present state of the image. Here is part of their description of the face:

> We noticed, at the left side of the forehead, a drop larger than the others and longer; it winds in a wave; the eyebrows appear well-formed; the eyes a bit less defined; the nose, being the most prominent part of the face, is well marked; the mouth is well-composed, it is quite small; the cheeks, swollen and disfigured, show well enough that they had been cruelly struck, particularly the right; the beard is neither too long nor too little, in the fashion of the Nazareans; it is thin in some places . . .[20]

It is possible that the intensity of the stains is decreasing with age. Luckily, modern photographic techniques more than compensate for this if so. The stains are revealed on photographic prints with a precision yielding far more detailed information to modern researchers than was available to any previous investigators.

But before considering the man represented by the stains, the nature of the stains themselves will be examined.

References

1. Sox, H. D., *File on the Shroud,* Coronet Books, Hodder and Stoughton, 1978, p. 84.
2. Wilson, I., *The Turin Shroud,* Gollancz, 1978, p. 1.
3. Gilbert, R. and M. M., 'Ultraviolet-visible reflectance and fluorescence spectra of the Shroud of Turin', *Applied Optics,* Vol. 19, No. 12, 15 June 1980, p. 1935.
4. Tyrer, J., 'Notes upon the Turin Shroud as a Textile', *General Report and Proceedings of the British Society for the Turin Shroud,* Autumn 1979-Summer 1981, p. 25.
5. Raes, G., Appendix B – Analysis Report, *Report of the Turin Commission on the Holy Shroud,* 1976, p. 83.
6. Tyrer, J., op. cit., p. 30.
7. Wilcox, R. K., *Shroud,* Corgi Books, 1978, p. 45.
8. Tyrer, J., 'Looking at the Turin Shroud as a Textile', *Textile Horizons,* December 1981, p. 20.
9. Humber, T., *The Fifth Gospel,* Pocket Books, 1974, p. 28.
10. Walsh, J., *The Shroud,* Star Books, W. H. Allen, 1979, p. 101.

11. Sox, H. D., *The Image on the Shroud,* Unwin Paperbacks, 1981, p. 76.
12. Tyrer, J., op. cit. (8), p. 21.
13. Stevenson, K. E. and G. R. Habermas, *Verdict on the Shroud,* Robert Hale, 1982, p. 26.
14. Rinaldi, P. M., *The Man in the Shroud,* Futura, 1974, p. 58.
15. Schwalbe, L. A. and R. N. Rogers, 'Physics and Chemistry of the Shroud of Turin', *Analytica Chimica Acta,* 135 (1982), 3-49, p. 44.
16. Tyrer, J., op. cit. (4), p. 25.
17. Walsh, J., op. cit., p. 30.
18. Wilson, I., op. cit., p. 11.
19. Ibid, p. 9.
20. Crispino, D., 'The Report of the Poor Clare Nuns, Chambery, 1532', *Shroud Spectrum International No 2,* Indiana Center for Shroud Studies, March 1982, p. 24.

Two
THE STAINS

At first sight all the stains, which appear to show the front and back of a wounded man, are the same colour. Only in sunlight is there an obvious difference. Then the marks of blood from his wounds can be seen to be of a red-carmine, quite different from the sepia within the outlines of his body.[1] There is another big difference between the two types of stain. The body-marks, and they will be called that or body-stains in future, reside only on the topmost fibres of the threads, whereas the blood-marks have soaked in between the gaps in the weave and also appear on the back of the cloth.

Looking at the Shroud under normal lighting, these points cannot be seen, and there are two other properties of the images that are invisible to the eye, and therefore of great importance. They are significant because if the image was painted, which would seem to be the most likely explanation, it would have been done for viewing by the naked eye, so any other property is unlikely.

The first property was discovered in 1898 when the earliest photographs were taken. When the photographer, Secundo Pia, developed the first plates, he was astonished to find that in the negative the image was incredibly lifelike. The body-stains, which to the eye seem comparatively disjointed,

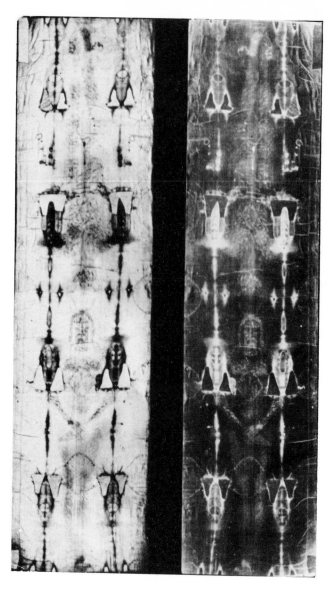

The Shroud with its normal tones, on the left, and with them reversed in a photographic negative, on the right.

take on an entity, a realism, that is uncanny. It is also very significant, for if a painter is asked to paint a portrait as a negative, and then his attempt is reversed by photography, it never looks as effective as a straightforward portrait in the correct tones. Besides which, what motive could a painter have had for doing it in this way, when his masterpiece could not be appreciated until photography was invented many centuries later?

There is a second property the image has which no painter would have given it. The stains contain three dimensional information. This was suggested for the first time by a Frenchman, Paul Vignon, working from Pia's photographs at the beginning of the century. He realized that the cloth was stained where it was not in contact with the man's body, and the closer it was to the body, the darker the stain. This could not be tested experimentally until the 1970s, when it was done by two USAF captains, Jackson and Jumper. They persuaded a friend of as near the right size and shape as possible to lie on a table. By photographing him from the side uncovered, and then covered with a length of cloth, they were able to determine the closeness of the cloth to his skin along the profile. They next measured the darkness of the stain on the Shroud along the same line, using an instrument called a micro-densitometer. When they plotted the darkness of the stain against the distance of the cloth from the body, it gave a neat curve, showing a precise relationship. The darkness of the Shroud at any point increased with its closeness to the skin, just as Vignon had suggested.

The Shroud can therefore be considered to have three-dimensional information, the z-axis figure being given by the darkness of the stain. This was demonstrated beautifully in 1976 by Jackson and Mottern, when a black-and-white print of the Shroud was viewed with a VP-8 Image Analyser. If a picture having this information of the third-dimensional values is studied with it, the object can be viewed not simply from straight ahead, but also from the sides. To Jackson's and Mottern's delight this is what happened, and they were able to obtain views of the man seen in the body-marks like semi-profiles.

The significance of this is very great. A normal

photograph or painting does not contain this information at all, and in the Image Analyser will look entirely unreal when an attempt is made to look at it from the side. There are some pictures that do have this property. For instance, a space craft landing on a planet that takes a photograph with the light coming from a source beside the camera will have this information: the nearer the object to the light and camera, the brighter it will appear; in this way rocks and boulders can be viewed using the VP-8 Image Analyser as if they were three-dimensional. It is very difficult indeed to obtain such pictures on earth, but in fact phosphorescent objects photographed through light-attenuating media (a fog is one) give satisfactory results.[2]

The investigation of the stains was carried a great deal further in 1978. True, quite a lot of work had been done previously, but it had been piecemeal, often by scientists chosen on religious grounds. In 1978, after the public exhibition, teams of Italian and American scientists were allowed a week in which to carry out any tests they wished, provided they were non-destructive. The authorities had taken a great deal of persuading to allow the exhibition as well as the scientific examination, and this was a chance which it was felt might not occur again for a very long time.

The American team, called the Shroud of Turin Research Project, which gives a rather ugly acronym STURP, consisted of about thirty high-level scientists with over 8000 pounds weight of valuable equipment. The frame in which the cloth was to be suspended for the week alone cost $20,000 to construct, and much of the other apparatus was very expensive.

In the days available, the observations of the cloth included direct microscopic observations and photomacrographs, X-ray fluorescence spectrometry, low energy X-radiography, infra-red, visible and ultra-violet reflectance spectra, photo-electric and photographic fluorescence, direct macroscopic visual observations and photographic images in different known wavelength regions, as well as thermal emission images for a variety of wavelengths. Visual transmission, side-lit, and glancing angle photographs were also taken. Material vacuumed from the cloth was examined by electron microscopy and microprobe. Lastly, adhesive tape was applied to the cloth in various areas for later examination by a variety of techniques.[3] All this included 30,000 separate photographs.

Such an array of weaponry could be expected to produce conclusive results when applied to the unknown features of the cloth. Unfortunately, this has not happened. Partly this is because of the unsatisfactory conditions under which the team had to work. The palace gallery used for the tests was not suitable as a laboratory, having polished wood floors, a highly decorated baroque ceiling and anything but a clinical atmosphere. The nearest gentlemen's lavatory had to be made into the darkroom. There were guards appointed to watch every move made by the scientists, who had no idea how long they would be given to carry out experiments and so could not plan thoroughly.[4] Also, some tests with light or X-rays coming through the cloth, were partly spoilt because the backing could not be removed.

But even taking these complications into account, it is surprising that as a result of all the scientists' efforts the situation is as confusing as it ever was. Conclusive results were hoped for, with a consensus view from the scientists. However the STURP team has been quite unable to produce a formal, agreed report. Instead, groups of members of the team have published articles in various scientific journals specializing in their particular fields. The observations they have reported have been valuable, but their interpretations have caused major differences and considerable argument. Not only have the Americans on and off the team quarrelled, but the Americans and Italians have been just as opposed. At one stage the Italians let it be known that they had proved that the blood-marks on the cloth had originated from real blood, and the Americans were reported as fiercely criticizing this, saying that such a result was impossible. A little time later the STURP team came out with the same conclusion.

One important factor contributed to the lack of satisfactory results: the composition of the STURP team. It more or less selected itself, the members being mainly pure scientists with little or no experience in dealing with medieval relics. Had scientific experts from museums been included, much more might have been accomplished.

Before summarizing some of their results, the terms thread, fibre and fibril should be defined. The threads woven into the cloth are quite fine, about one-seventh of a millimetre wide.[5] However, each thread is spun from a hundred or more separate fibres.[6] When a stretch of fibre is separated, by adhering to a piece of adhesive tape for instance, it is called a fibril.

Some of the more important results the STURP team obtained were:

1. Under the microscope, the body-image can be seen to be discontinuous and consists of the yellowing of fibres on the tops of the threads of the cloth. The colouration only goes a maximum of two or three fibres deep into the thread structure. The darkness of the stain depends on how many fibres are yellowed; in other words the number of coloured fibres per unit area. The affected fibres are coloured to the same extent.

2. Thirty-two adhesive tape samples were removed from a variety of areas on the cloth. It was noticed that the tape came off more easily from non-image than image areas, suggesting that the latter were in some way weakened. There were significantly more yellow fibrils from image areas than non-image, suggesting that they are the dominant visible image element. However, McCrone and Skirius reported that eighteen of the tapes showed sub-micrometre red particles they identified as Fe_2O_3 of varying degrees of hydration. They found that none of the non-image areas contained these particles, suggesting that they may be a red pigment that was applied to the cloth either to strengthen the existing image or create it. More will be said of this later. In addition to Fe_2O_3, Heller and Adler found 'blood sherds' and 'blood flakes' on many of the samples. The 'blood flakes' are nearly indistinguishable from the Fe_2O_3 particles optically.

3. Fluorescence tests showed that the plain linen background fluoresced, and the light scorch marks gave a faint reddish brown. However, there was no fluorescence

from the body-marks or the blood-marks.

4. The stain-density cloth-body-distance correlation, demonstrated by the VP-8 Image Analyser using the Enrie black-and-white photographs, worked also with the new colour photographs and black-and-white photographs taken on panchromatic film.

5. There was no alteration of the image area as it approached the parts of the cloth charred by the 1532 fire. As the silver casket in which the Shroud was stored would probably have melted at 820-850°C, changes should have been detectable had organic dyes or stains been used. Most of the inorganic pigments available during the fourteenth century would also have altered.

6. The water used to extinguish the fire migrated through scorched and unscorched image areas, and no part of the image was apparently water-soluble. The movement of the water was retarded by blood-marks however.[7]

7. The blood-marks are quite different, thread fibres being matted and cemented together with signs of granules. Red-orange encrustations can be seen between the fibres and in the crevices, with higher concentrations in the valleys at the intersections of warp and weft threads. In places it looks as if such material has fallen away or been rubbed off, leaving exposed the red-orange fibres beneath. The various tests give sufficient evidence to assume the marks were caused by real blood. One interesting result is that some of the blood areas have small fluorescent haloes. These might have been from serum that separated from the blood.

8. There was a considerable amount of 'dirt' on the footprint on the cloth.

Having presented their observations, the scientists could attempt an explanation, and this was where the difficulty lay. On the evidence, the STURP team deduced that the image did not contain coloured foreign matter. They acknowledged that there was possibly a connection between the presence of

Fe_2O_3 particles and the image, but felt such a conclusion unjustified from the few tape samples. They did not deny the particles were there, but felt that they might well have been 'blood flakes' from the blood-mark areas spread when the cloth was folded.

The only explanation of the image formation they felt to be credible, in view of all the experimental results, was that the chemical composition of the cellulose fabric of the linen had been changed in some way. The nearest approach to the effect of the Shroud image they obtained was by treating some fresh linen with thin coatings of perspiration, olive oil, myrrh and aloes and then baking it gently to simulate ageing. The problem arises as to how the gentle gradation came on the cloth, for if by simple contact, there would have been outlined contrast. An ingenious additional suggestion that sought to explain the three-dimensional information was that the stiff cloth was only in contact with the high points on the body when first applied. Water vapour from the body slowly softened it, until it lay in contact with the whole surface. The stains would have varied if they had been dependent on the time of contact. Unfortunately, this still does not explain why the image did not diffuse through the cloth. It is also extraordinary that the cloth was finally in contact everywhere, in view of the considerable hollows of a normal face. And why, if it depended on the time, was the darkness of the thread stain unaltered, simply the number per unit area?

Some points were undoubtedly achieved. The team felt sure the blood-marks had indeed been caused by blood. They had a good idea of what the image was, and were confident it did not consist of foreign matter, and was not the work of a forger. *How* it had been formed was another matter.

At the same time the Italian scientists were analyzing their observations and continuing their research. Their most important results came from analysis of the blood-marks, for not only were they able to show that the marks must have been formed by human blood, later confirmed by the STURP team, but they also determined its group, AB.[8]

There is nothing very newsworthy in these conclusions, and their impact was lessened by their scattered publication. All the hard work of these many scientists in their several fields barely hit the headlines, which was a pity. What was well publicized was the view of one man, not in the team, who based his opinion on one technique, microscopy, in which he had a well-deserved reputation. But the view he expressed was clear, and newsworthy. It was that the Shroud is a fake, painted in the fourteenth century. Here was the sensation, and he was the investigator who was persistently interviewed when the subject was mentioned on the British media. His argument needs to be examined.

References

1. *The Report of the Turin Commission on the Holy Shroud,* 1976, p. 20.
2. Schwalbe, L. A., and R. N. Rogers, 'Physics and Chemistry of the Shroud of Turin', *Analytica Chimica Acta,* 135 (1982), 3-49, p. 7.
3. Ibid, p. 10.
4. Sox, H. D., *The Image on the Shroud,* Unwin Paperbacks, 1981, p. 90.
5. Schwalbe, L. A., and R. N. Rogers, op. cit., p. 43.
6. Ibid., p. 11.
7. Ibid., pp. 22-24.
8. Bollone, Jorio and Massaro, 'Identification of the Group of the Traces of Human Blood on the Shroud', *Shroud Spectrum International No. 6,* Indiana Center for Shroud Studies, March 1983.

Three

FORGED OR GENUINE?

If the piece of cloth was painted, it was almost certainly done in the fourteenth century. A bishop of Troyes in France, Pierre d'Arcis, was concerned because the cloth was being venerated by people in his see, although he was sure it had been painted. A predecessor in his post had investigated it. He wrote to his pope, Clement VII, about it in 1389. His letter includes the following.

> The Lord Henry of Poitiers, of pious memory, then Bishop of Troyes . . . set himself earnestly to work to fathom the truth of this matter . . . Eventually, after diligent inquiry and examination, he discovered the fraud and how the said cloth had been cunningly painted, the truth being attested by the artist who had painted it, to wit, that it was a work of human skill and not miraculously wrought or bestowed. Accordingly, after taking mature counsel with wise theologians and men of the law, seeing that he neither ought nor could allow the matter to pass, he began to institute formal proceedings against the said Dean and his accomplices in order to root out this false persuasion. They, seeing their wickedness discovered, hid away the said cloth so that the Ordinary could not find it, and they kept it hidden afterwards for thirty-four years or thereabouts down to the present year.[1]

Strong evidence, and if the cloth really was painted, this would have happened not long before 1355.

One or two qualifications have been expressed about the letter which should be borne in mind. Firstly, the Bishop wrote it in a very angry mood. Permission to exhibit the cloth in Lirey, about twelve miles from Troyes, had been obtained from the papal legate instead of him, the bishop. The reason is not known, but it may well have been because of the previous animosity between the canons and the bishop, so that he would have played any card he could to defeat them. His description of his predecessor's actions seems surprising, since the former bishop gave his confirmation of the establishment of the church in Lirey on 28 May 1356, bestowing his unqualified and lavish blessings. This would have been after his discovery that the cloth venerated there was a forgery. Note also that the Pope, in response to Bishop d'Arcis's letter, did not stop the exhibition, but insisted on two occasions that the bishop remain 'perpetually silent' on the matter. If the former bishop did locate an artist who claimed to have painted the Shroud, there is a possibility that he had painted one of the other shrouds that were venerated in Europe at the time. There were plenty of them.

Such historical problems cannot be cleared up, nor do they particularly matter. It is not just the letter quoted that makes many historians say the cloth must be a fake. They also deduce this because for many centuries its location is entirely unknown. To a scientist that is no proof whatsoever that it cannot be genuine. If an old pot is dug up, a painting found in an attic, an ancient scroll in a Jerusalem bazaar, the items are examined by experts scientifically. If, as a result of the most careful tests, the pot is pronounced to be Roman, the painting an unrecorded Rembrandt, the scroll one from the Essene community beside the Dead Sea, no one says 'They can't be! We have no idea who the owners have been for centuries. They have no history whatsoever. Therefore they are fakes!' The same standards should be applied to the Shroud. Examine the material, analyze the stains, and let the cloth tell its story.

It is interesting that Dr Walter McCrone is the scientist involved in doubting the authenticity of the Shroud, for he

was involved in a classic examination of a similar kind some
years ago.[2] In 1957 an American book dealer bought from an
Italian bookseller in Barcelona a map, known as the Vinland
Map. It was apparently drawn by a monk from the Upper
Rhine during the fifteenth century, and it showed that Leif
Ericson probably visited America about 500 years before
Columbus. It was extremely authentic in appearance, and
wormholes in it exactly matched those in two well-known
medieval documents, suggesting that it had been bound with
them. After Yale University bought it, they sent it to the
British Museum for non-destructive testing, and it was
found that the map did not quench fluorescence under
ultra-violet light as the other two documents did. So the map
was sent to Dr McCrone for further testing. Removing less
than a microgram he discovered that while the parchment
was genuinely of medieval date, the ink contained a
synthesized pigment, anatase, not developed until about
1920. The map was a fraud.

And now Dr McCrone was claiming the Shroud image
was painted. What was the evidence?

Dr McCrone was able to study 32 tape samples brought
back by the STURP team from the 1978 examination. The
tapes had been pressed against the cloth in many different
places, including unaffected linen background, scorch areas,
body-marks and blood-marks. As a result of his examination, he was soon saying that the Shroud image has two
constituents: uniformly coloured linen fibres and iron
particles. The nature and origin of the coloured fibres was
unknown, but the iron oxide was a mixture of red and
yellow pigment particles (pure Fe_2O_3 and hydrous Fe_2O_3
respectively). None of the control samples, where there was
no image, showed these red particles, whereas all the
blood-mark ones did as well as two-thirds of the body-mark
ones. He concluded that there was a direct correlation
between Fe_2O_3 particle concentrations and image areas, and
suggested that they had been intentionally added during the
past 200 years. To demonstrate how the iron oxide would
have been applied to the cloth without any of the directional
indications that are obtained with brush strokes, McCrone
rubbed his finger in some powdered jeweller's rouge,

transferred it to a piece of paper until there was very little indeed left on his finger, and then used that to apply to a piece of linen.[3]

His claim caused considerable opposition from the STURP team and Turin. He did not retract in the least, but gave a clear description of his methods and findings, and revealed further conclusions. The iron oxide particles were now reckoned much more like the artist's pigment known as Venetian or Indian red than the jeweller's rouge. Not only that, but they were very closely attached to the fibres, sometimes in clumps within a transparent gel. Applying the agent amido black, he obtained a fine blue stain round these clumps of oxide. This indicated a protein material had been used as a weak medium, a tempera made from collagen. As he found this on the body-mark and blood-mark areas, he concluded it must have been put there by man. To account for the three-dimensional information, Dr McCrone suggested that the artist tried to portray a shroud, rather than a portrait of a man, so formed the image by working from the contact points where the cloth would have touched the skin.

In conclusion Dr McCrone stated:

> Our work now supports the two Bishops and it seems reasonable that the image was painted on the cloth shortly before the first exhibition, about 1357. It is, however, possible that the image and/or the cloth is at least as old as about 1350, that it was done by an artist and that if all iron earth pigment plus tempera medium were removed there would be no image on the 'Shroud'.

The STURP team did not agree at all with Dr McCrone's conclusions, and they were using a very wide range of techniques.[4] Two members of the team, Heller and Adler, studied the fibrils with a microscope as Dr McCrone had done, and their observations were different. They reported on the modern debris with the fibrils – insect parts, wax, modern synthetic fibrils, red and blue silk, wool and flair tip pen dye marks. The red and blue silk fibrils were seen with almost every sample, and presumably came from backing cloths with frequent folding and unfolding. As has been mentioned, they also found 'blood sherds' and 'blood flakes' on many of the samples, which were almost indistinguishable from the comparably-sized Fe_2O_3 particles optically, so the possibility arose of mistaken identity. There could have been a dispersion of these blood remains whenever the cloth was folded and unfolded, spreading the particles to other areas.[5]

There were many other tests, and some of Dr McCrone's conclusions were criticized. His amido black test had been positive only for the blood-mark areas, for instance, so that there was no clear indication that protein-based tempera was on the body image. Nor is amido black the best test, according to others, as it stains cellulose so easily that false positive results may occur. The further tests carried out by STURP members showed that the discolouration of the yellow fibrils did not come from any likely organic or inorganic pigmentation. The STURP team's conclusion that there was no pigment on the cloth was derived from a far wider selection of analytical methods, and this must be placed against Dr McCrone's clear mastery and superior experience in his own field.

This argument of the scientists whether the cloth was painted or not is on a very narrow plane, and the artistic considerations and the force of common sense should also enter the lists.

The common sense view in favour of painting is one most people form when first hearing of the cloth. Surely it cannot be two thousand years old, as it is claimed to be? Most likely it was painted for some religious purpose in medieval times, when relics were being produced by the hundred. Since there were more than forty purported shrouds around, this one is probably as false as the rest.

However, the arguments against the cloth having been painted are remarkably powerful. Some of them are:

1. The painting is so faint, the gradation cannot be seen when close enough to paint it. Only by standing some feet back can its effect be seen.

2. The anatomy of the body is perfect, right down to

small details like the separation of serum from blood.

3. The blood-marks were caused by real blood. Also the fibres underneath them are not stained yellow. The blood-marks were therefore applied to the cloth first and prevented the body-stains from appearing there. An artist would have applied the blood-marks last.

4. No medieval artist would have been able to, nor did he have any reason to, paint a *negative* image which would give a perfect positive on reversal centuries later when photography enabled this to be seen.

5. A medieval artist would have used a brush, and the direction of the brushmarks would be detectable with a microscope. No directions of brushmarks can be seen.

6. No painting has the three-dimensional information revealed by the VP-8 Image Analyser.

7. A European artist would not have troubled to obtain linen that could only have been made in the Middle East, and had pollen on its surface from exposure there.

8. There are details in the stains which must have resulted from details of crucifixion not known by medieval artists. (The position of the nail wound, no sign of thumbs and the use of a *sedile* on the cross – covered in the next three chapters.)

9. Medieval painters, and indeed nearly all painters up to the middle of the nineteenth century,[6] worked from outlines, whereas the Shroud contains an extraordinarily soft gradation from image to background.

10. Medieval paints would have cracked on folding and changed nature close to the heat of the 1532 fire.

11. The material appears to support itself fairly stiffly between the knees, hands and abdomen, and across the hollow between the chest and chin. On the other hand there is more contact widthways around the arms, legs and body. The drape is stiffer lengthways, along the warp, than widthways, along the weft. To a materials expert[7] it

would be astonishing for an artist to represent drape so correctly.

12. The presence of dirt where the bottom of the foot is represented is an unlikely touch of realism for a painting.

The case rests. As the arguments stand at the moment, those maintaining that the cloth could not have been painted seem to have a far stronger case. But, if it was not painted, some natural process must have caused the stains.

References

1. Wilson, I., *The Turin Shroud,* Gollancz, 1978, p. 230.
2. Sox, H. D., *The Image on the Shroud,* Unwin Paperbacks, 1981, p. 20.
3. Ibid., p. 34.
4. Schwalbe, L. A., and R. M. Rogers, 'Physics and Chemistry of the Shroud of Turin', *Analytica Chimica Acta,* 135 (1982), 3-49, pp. 11-16.
5. Heller, J. H., and A. D. Adler, 'A Chemical Investigation of the Shroud of Turin', *Canadian Journal of Forensic Science,* Vol. 14, No. 3 (1981), pp. 81-100.
6. Wilson, I., op. cit., p. 10.
7. Tyrer, J., 'Notes upon the Turin Shroud as a Textile', *General Report and Proceedings of the British Society for the Turin Shroud,* Autumn 1979-Summer 1981, p. 29.

Four
A NATURAL PROCESS?

Paul Vignon has already been mentioned as the man who first suggested that the darkness of the stain decreased with the distance of the cloth from the skin. He did his research just after the turn of the century, using the first photographs ever taken of the cloth, and the full account of his work then can be read in his book *The Shroud of Christ*, published in 1902.

Vignon's first move was to go to Turin to meet the photographer, Secundo Pia. He had to be satisfied that the photographs had not been faked in any way, and could be used as scientific evidence. Once he was certain this was so, he returned to France to study large positives and negatives in detail.

The major marks on the cloth have already been mentioned. They are the scorches and patches from the 1532 fire, and the stains caused by the front and back of a man's body, on which can be seen blood-marks from his injuries. Closer examination of the photographs reveals many important details.

The face is best seen on the negative, for with the tones reversed it is remarkably life-like. The man has a thin, rather old face, his hair coming down each side, with a majestic expression. The left side of his face looks rather buffeted,

A Piece of Cloth

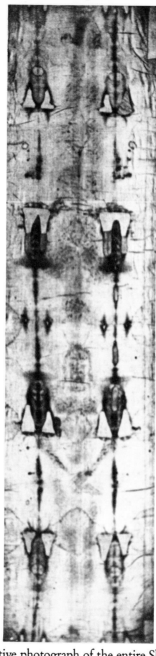

A positive photograph of the entire Shroud.

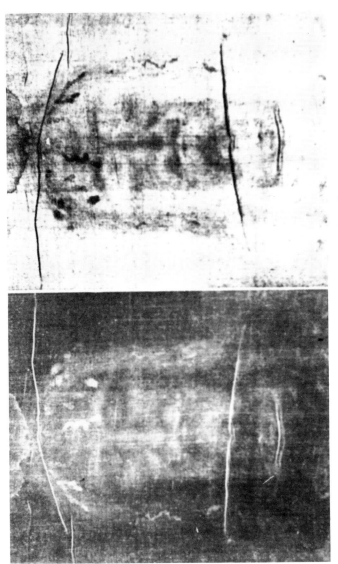

Negative and positive images of the face.

particularly just below the eye, and his nose appears swollen
on one side. The streaks of blood are better seen in the
positive. The most obvious one, just above the left eyebrow,
has the shape of a 3 (reversed in the positive) with an extra
drop just below its base. Other streaks of blood come down
the hair, and they are all round the head, a cluster of them
clearly visible on the back image.

The main blood-marks on the body are on the forearms,
the left wrist, a big one on the right side of the chest running
into a patch from the fire, a series of trickles going right
across the back above waist height, under the soles of the feet
on the rear image and on toes on the front image. The
wounds on the hand and feet suggest the man suffered
crucifixion. The blood-marks on the left hand are in the
shape of a V, the point issuing from a place on the wrist
rather than the hand itself. Under the feet the blood
apparently issued from the middle of the soles, some blood
running to the toes, presumably when he was suspended
upright, and some to the heels when the body was laid down.
There is a jagged blood-mark on the cloth beside the right
heel.

The body-marks are delicately shaded, and match the
shape of a body except for a few details. The shoulders and
neck do not appear on the front image, perhaps because the
cloth was held too far away from them, and the same is true
for the bottoms of the shins. The right wrist is obscured by
the left one which covered it, and although the fingers on
both hands can be seen clearly, neither thumb is there. The
left shoulder-blade appears rather dark, as if rubbed or
bruised. But the main surface marks are shaped like small
dumb-bells, and they can be seen all over the back, buttocks
and legs, and even on the front image in places. It has been
suggested that these are scourge-marks.

The victim must have died before the fourth century,
when crucifixion was finally outlawed in the Roman Empire,
and men were usually scourged before being nailed to
crosses. The Roman *flagrum* used for this had a short handle,
with several long thongs or chains attached. Near the end of
these thongs were fixed pieces of bone or lumps of lead, to
bruise and bite into the flesh, adding to the agony and

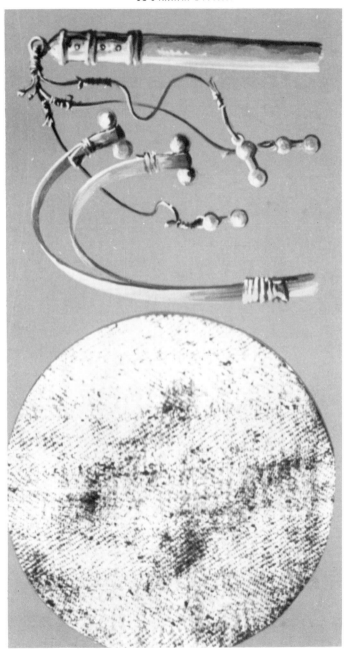

A dumb-bell shaped bruise and the type of Roman flagrum which probably inflicted the wound.

weakening effect. Two of these, wielded by men on each side of him, could have made the marks seen on the man in the Shroud.

Vignon felt at first that the image might have been painted, but the realism of the negative argued against this. Apart from the difficulty of working in reverse, why should a medieval painter have attempted it when the worth of his art could not be appreciated for many centuries? But Vignon realized there was also the possibility an artist had painted it normally, but in time chemistry had altered the paints, reversing their tones as had happened to a fresco in Assisi. In that particular case sulphur had acted on the lead base of the paints causing this inversion; but in the case of the Shroud the image is of one colour only, so Vignon concluded that this explanation would not be possible. In addition, inversion could only occur with solid paint, and there was no evidence of any paint on the cloth at all.

Vignon found further evidence against painting in the blood-marks. They are clearly outlined. A liquid placed on the cloth would have spread along the threads, leaving jagged edges, so that a forger would have used either thick paint for the blood, which would have come off with frequent folding and unfolding, or some sort of stain, which was unlikely if not absurd.

Vignon, the biologist, next studied the blood-mark above the left eyebrow. It starts with a wound not far below the hair.

Vignon's section through a drop of blood which has dried on an impermeable surface.

The blood which has flowed therefrom has met in its course the two wrinkles of the forehead, and has, by this slight opposition, been forced to spread itself out, forming two small horizontal pools; thence it continued to flow, until it ended in a tear of blood close to the eyebrow, and having thus flowed, it dried upon the skin.

Now any drop of blood, drying thus, upon a substance into which it does not penetrate here, takes, when coagulated, a sort of basin-like shape, a section of which we give here.

The border or brim of the basin is formed by the fibrine of the blood, containing the red corpuscles in its coagulum; the centre is composed of the serum, which in drying takes a dull brown tint. Here, as the liquid part of the serum evaporates, the convexity of the centre is depressed. The contour of the drop of blood preserves, however, the same shape as when it was fresh.

Now this description applied exactly to the blood-drop on the forehead.[1]

Vignon studied the other blood-marks, and found further evidence that the accuracy of the image was astonishing, and far beyond the knowledge of any painter in medieval times. Vignon felt this particularly applied to the blood-mark on the left hand.

The nail-wound of the left hand is in the wrist, *not* in the centre of the palm as demanded by tradition. In a forged relic such a parade of independence would scarcely have been tolerated. As it was, to have shown the public only one hand, and consequently only one wound, was remarkable enough. Such licences would be pardoned only in the most authentic relic. Yet anatomy proves that the nails *must* have been driven into the wrists, *not* into the hands. Here again tradition is contradicted.

What would have become of the body on the cross, had the nails been driven through the palms of the hands? The weight of the body would quickly have enlarged the wounds, and the ligaments at the base of the fingers would soon have given away. If, however, the nails were driven in at the wrist there would be no chance of the wound's enlargement; indeed the very weight of the body would throw pressure on the extremities of the metacarpal bones, which are very firmly united.[2]

Vignon describes this feature with a scientist's exactness,

and may have felt no one had noticed it before him. Surprisingly, it was mentioned as early as 1598, in the first book written about the cloth. The author, Monsignor Palleotto, described how the nail went through the hand at the spot 'where the hand and forearm join, known to the doctors as the carpus'. He also pointed out that nailing through the palms would not have been possible as 'they would not sustain the weight of the body, but would tear, as is confirmed by the experience of painters and sculptors who have studied corpses'.[3] Painters of the Renaissance had the knowledge to paint it correctly, and indeed Van Dyck and Rubens are among those who showed nails going through the wrists of the crucified victim, so this particular detail cannot be used as a strong argument against forgery later than approximately 1400.

The narrowness of the face image interested Vignon, and also the way the hair was held up beside the cheeks, and he suggested there must have been cushions or similar supports placed one each side of the head. In that case the cloth would not have fallen round the edges of the cheeks, which would have given a wider image, as he illustrated with a diagram.

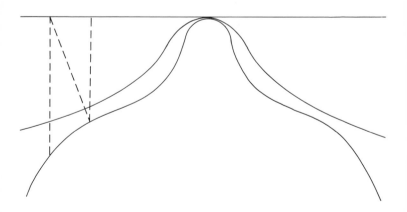

Vignon's section, showing how the face, even when the cloth is held flat, appears narrow.

Apart from holding the hair up, it would also account for the way the shoulders do not appear in the front image, for those same cushions would have held the cloth away from them.

Vignon's detailed description of how the stains in particular areas were formed makes fascinating reading. But Vignon is best known for his attempts to discover the general process by which they were transferred to the cloth.

Once he had eliminated painting as a method of forging, he wondered whether a live body could have been used. Wearing a false beard, he put red chalk on his skin and lay on a laboratory bench. His assistants then placed on him a length of linen coated with albumen and attempted to pick up the chalk impression of his body. The results were grotesque compared with the original. Nor was there any way of obtaining a delicate gradation. If the cloth did not touch the body at any point, nothing was picked up there. The skin could not transfer the solid to the cloth across a space.

It was this that fascinated Vignon. He did manage to obtain a negative by this method, but a very rough and coarse one, whereas the print on the shroud

is a still more perfect negative, because the image has been also in part produced *without* contact. Nevertheless we do not pretend that this negative is as true a one as if it had been taken by means of a lens . . . In the language of science it is the result of *action at a distance* (that is to say without contact); geometrically speaking it is a *protection*.[4]

This action over a distance meant that the stains could not have resulted from the transfer of a solid or a liquid from the skin to the cloth. It had to be a gas. So Vignon, and a colleague, Rene Colson, set out to find what gas it could have been.

They first investigated oriental burial habits and found that aromatic substances, especially myrrh and aloes, were pounded up in pure olive oil for use as an unguent. This could have coated the cloth. Experiment showed that when the gas ammonia came in contact with the treated cloth, just the right colour stains were formed in time. They then had to find out when a body can give off ammonia.

Ammonia occurs as a final product of the fermentation of urea. Urea is mainly discharged by the body in urine. That is why mothers are affected by the pungent fumes of ammonia when they change wet nappies that have been worn by their babies for some time. But urea is also discharged in very small quantities in perspiration.

Normally there would be too little urea exuded to have any effect, but Vignon was delighted to find:

> that *in morbid sweat* the increase of urea is quite astonishing. M. Gautier says: 'Urea may be produced so abundantly in certain morbid sweats that it forms crystals on the surface of the body. A fringe of such crystals has been seen on the forehead where it joins the hair, presenting an appearance like down' . . . M. Gautier also personally assured me that viscous sweat strongly charged with urea would be given off by any fever patient in a crisis of pain. Further – and this is of great importance – a man who has been tortured for a length of time will at death be found to have his body covered with a deposit rich in urea. This deposit left after the heavy sweating, caused by acute pain, has somewhat evaporated. The skin would remain moist. If, then, after death such a corpse were covered with a sheet soaked in aloes, the urea would ferment, carbonate of ammonia would be produced, ammoniacal vapours would arise; these vapours would oxidise the aloes, and would reproduce on the cloth a negative by chemical action.[5]

It seemed to tie up very well. There were some slight snags. Vignon tried to use this process to obtain a reasonable stain on cloth from a plaster head of Michelangelo and failed. However, he did manage a good one of a hand if he let the ammonia filter up through a glove, but why the glove was necessary was not clear. But the chemistry seemed to fit in so well, and the abnormal exudation of urea in the sweat of a tortured man was such an extraordinary coincidence, that Vignon's *vaporographic* theory, as he called it, had considerable support after his book was published. The doubts came later.

References

1. Vignon, P., *The Shroud of Christ,* Constable, 1902, p. 29.
2. Ibid, p. 40.
3. Hynek, R. W., *The True Likeness,* Sheed and Ward, 1951, p. 52.
4. Vignon, P., op. cit., p. 137.
5. Ibid., p. 169.

Five

THE
THERMOGRAPHIC
CORRECTION

The vaporographic theory of Vignon seems very persuasive. The extraordinary way in which ammonia can be produced by the body from urea under duress seems such a coincidence that it must surely be true. But there are snags, and the theory soon lost favour.

The first problem is caused by the gradation. The logic that the agent must be a gas rather than a liquid or solid, since it acts over a distance rather than by contact, seems incontestable. However, if it is a gas, how does its effect decrease with the distance to the cloth?

The volume of gas between the body and the cloth would be comparatively small. Any gas emitted by the body would soon become of uniform density in that volume, the gas diffusing through the cloth at the same rate as it was generated on the skin. There would be no question of gentle gradation, therefore. Vapours diffusing through space do not travel in parallel lines, nor do their densities decrease with distance.[1] In view of the small volume between the cloth and the skin, the density of the gas would have been practically constant throughout the volume and so the stain would have been uniform: for instance, there would not have been the gentle gradation above the eyes.

The second main objection has also been indicated, for as

the gas diffused up through the cloth the reaction would have continued, whereas only the closest fibres of the closest threads have been stained.

The STURP team also eliminated the theory on less important grounds, principally because they could find no trace of the products expected from the ammonia-aloes reaction.

What they have not considered so far is that a condition might be added that could answer all the objections. That condition is that the body in the Shroud was at a *uniform temperature*, and a *higher temperature* than that of its surroundings.

This was first suggested to me as an answer to the problem by the East Midlands forensic scientists in Nottingham.[2] When asked to consider the photographs of the Shroud as if they were evidence of a contemporary crime, they reckoned one conclusion must be drawn from the stains. Although, prior to discovery of the function of the heart and the circulation of the blood in the seventeenth century, the body in the Shroud would have been certified as being absolutely dead, by the standards of our own time it was in a deep coma.

The grounds for their deduction were these. Any chemical staining reaction, whether ammonia-aloes or the action of some other agent on linen, would almost certainly have depended on temperature: the higher the temperature the darker the stain. For simple reactions a rule-of-thumb rule is that the rate of reaction doubles for every rise in temperature of ten Centigrade degrees. Photographers are aware of how a slightly higher temperature means that a film develops to the correct darkness in a shorter time, and cooks find that the few degrees higher cooking temperature obtained with a pressure cooker means that the time required is considerably less. The depth of staining over the length of the front and back of the body is fairly constant, so the temperature of the cloth must also have been approximately uniform. This could only happen if the blood were still circulating, the heart just beating. The body must have been in a coma, therefore, and not clinically dead by twentieth century standards.

As soon as a body dies, its heart stops beating, and the

blood is no longer forced round the body keeping the temperature nearly even. Very soon the extremities – feet, hands, nose – which have a large surface area compared with the matter they hold, cool down to the outside temperature. The trunk of the body and the head hold a very great deal of heat and will retain this for many hours. Not only that, but the blood, no longer kept circulating, will naturally fall through gravity, causing lividity on the bottom surface. Some of these places, the buttocks and shoulder-blades in a prone body for instance, would therefore stay warm even longer, so that the signs of that warmth should have been visible as darker areas on the Shroud.

Had it covered a dead body, the forensic experts would have expected no stain at all towards the feet, and the hands and nose would also have shown much less stain than they do. At the University of Leeds Department of Forensic Medicine they have videotaped bodies as they cool after death with thermographic cameras, and these effects can be seen clearly.[3]

In view of the fact that men get cold hands, feet and nose when they go out in cold weather, in spite of the circulation of their blood, it seems surprising that the man in the Shroud, in a state of coma with his heart only just beating, experienced so little change in temperature along the length of his body. Unfortunately, there are obvious reasons why scientific experiments with people's bodies in a state of coma are not easy to arrange, at any rate for someone not in the medical profession. Nor is it easy to find scientific papers that have investigated surface temperatures of live bodies. There is one that concerns experiments carried out in the New York Hospital in 1938. This found that the temperature along the body kept reasonably constant until the outside temperature fell more than five Centigrade degrees below the body temperature, when the temperature of the feet fell rapidly with the drop in temperature.[4] However, the people in the experiment were naked, and so they would have lost heat more rapidly, particularly as the skin would have evaporated freely. Under a cloth there would not have been this type of loss to any extent, and the cloth would also have cut down loss by convection and conduction, while radiation energy would have been partly reflected back. In view of the much lower rate of metabolism, the temperature could possibly have remained reasonably constant, provided the outside temperature in the tomb, assuming the body lay in the Shroud in a tomb, was not very low. On Easter Day 1981 a thermometer placed on the burial ledge in the Garden Tomb in Jerusalem at sunset read 22°C.

To see if the effect of a live body on a cloth covering it could be demonstrated, I obtained a linen sheet as near as possible to the published characteristics of the Shroud from the Lambeg Industrial Research Association of Northern Ireland. A mattress was placed on the floor, and a volunteer lay on it, breathing through a length of Bunsen burner tubing so that his breath would not warm the cloth all round his head. The sheet was placed on him for four minutes. After that time it was raised to the vertical, viewed both by a thermographic camera connected to the television monitor and videotape recorder and a 35mm camera. The body was beautifully outlined on the sheet by the thermographic camera, the image going the whole length of the body.

This evidence from the forensic scientists, that the body in the Shroud was in a coma rather than absolutely dead by twentieth century standards, could remove the barriers to Vignon's vaporographic theory.

There were two main problems. Firstly, since the gas would have been a uniform density all round the body under the cloth, there would have been a large area of general stain, with none of the gradation seen on the Shroud. The second problem was the existence of the stains on only the closest fibres, for the gas would have affected the cloth as it diffused through.

If the skin temperature is assumed to have been a constant, but, since the body was in a comatose state, higher than the temperature outside the cloth, both points could be explained. The temperature of the cloth at any point would depend on how close it was to the skin. Where it was in contact it would have been skin temperature; as it moved away it would get cooler until, beyond a certain distance, it would have been more or less the same as the outside temperature. It followed that the closer the cloth to the skin,

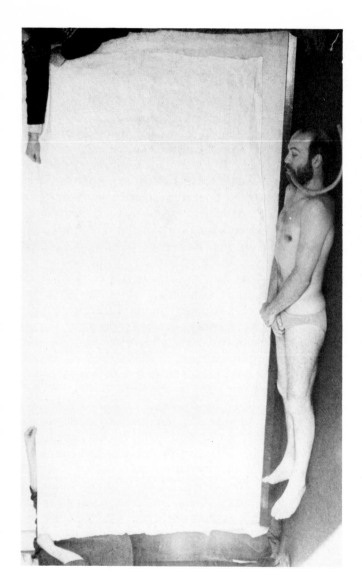

What a 35mm camera saw as the sheet was lifted up from the volunteer.

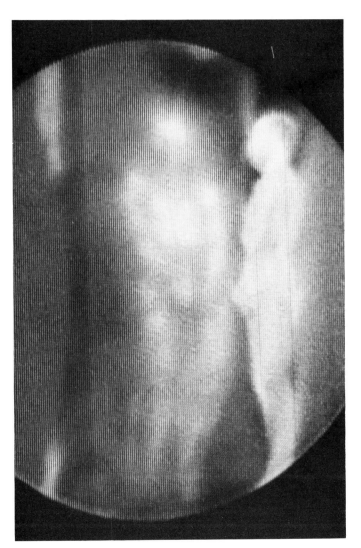

The same view as seen by the thermal imaging camera.

the higher the temperature. And, since the staining process was almost certain to have depended on the temperature, it follows that *the closer the cloth to the skin the darker the stain,* which is the three-dimensional information characteristic no other theory has managed to explain.

The second problem with the vaporographic theory may be answered bearing in mind the very low conductivity of still air. Air is an excellent insulator of heat provided it is kept still, which explains why men wear light, fluffy clothes that trap the air in their fibres and put foam in the cavities in house walls. When the sheet was placed on top of the body, convection and radiation between the skin and the cloth carried heat much more than conduction, so that although there was a temperature gradient across the air gap – which explains why the greater the gap, the greater the difference in temperature – the temperature dropped much more rapidly at the border of the linen. The STURP team also reported linen fibrils that were stained at one end and not at the other. There is no surprise in that either. Physics teachers can enliven their lessons with quite a few spectacular demonstrations, spectacular because they are surprising. One of these is to boil water in a paper container – a schoolchild's 'water-bomb' does admirably, particularly if you make it with wings to hold it by – on the flame of a Bunsen burner. Provided there is water inside, the paper shows no sign of scorching, even though it is held right down on the flame. It is an admirable demonstration of the insulating property of still air, for it is the air trapped in the fibrils of the paper pointing down into the flame that take the enormous temperature gradient between the flame and the paper-water mass. If you have never seen the experiment and do not think it works, try it. The way in which a fibril on the Shroud, broken so that it pointed down towards the body, was differentially stained along its length, should be clear.

The STURP team were also unhappy at not being able to find any trace of the chemicals they think would have remained in the cloth as a result of the ammonia-aloes reaction. They may be right. Vignon may have been incorrect in suggesting that particular reaction. That will not necessarily affect the issue. Suppose later experiments show that the presence of some other agent throughout the cloth during the time it wrapped the man's body caused the stains. The rate at which that agent worked, whatever it was, would have depended on the temperature at any point. Vignon's argument was perfectly correct in saying that the gas between the skin and the cloth must have caused the stain since the skin acted over a distance; but the gas could have been warm air! It was the air that carried the heat upwards and raised the temperature of the cloth, so that the stains seen there represent a temperature map.

The man in the Shroud must have been in a coma, therefore, and not dead. The main evidence for this is twofold; the evenness of the stains along the length of his body, and the three-dimensional information.

The question arises as to what happened to him then. He could have died completely, or he could have come round again within a reasonable time. If he died, his body must have been removed from the cloth shortly afterwards, for decomposition would have destroyed the cloth and the stains. Decomposition starts remarkably rapidly in the areas where the cloth was made, and burial must take place by law within twenty-four hours because of this. There is also the possibility that he recovered, his metabolic rate and temperature climbing up again to the normal and consciousness returning. However, this seems hardly likely when the stains showed he was scourged cruelly and then crucified. It depends on what precisely was involved in the process of crucifixion.

References

1. Stevenson, K. E., and G. R. Habermas, *Verdict on the Shroud,* Robert Hale, 1982, p. 89.
2. Hoare, R. P., *The Testimony of the Shroud,* Quartet, 1978, pp. 47-55.
3. Newitt, C., and M. A. Green, 'A Thermographic Study of Surface Cooling of Cadavers', *Journal of the Forensic Science Society* 19, 179 (1979), pp. 179-181.
4. Hardy, J. D., and E. F. Du Bois, 'Basal Metabolism, Radiation, Convection and Vaporization at Temperatures of 22

to 35°C', *The Journal of Nutrition,* Vol. 15, No. 5, (1938), pp. 480-486.

Six
CRUCIFIXION

Descriptions exist of crucified men being taken down from the cross and surviving. One is given by the Jewish historian Josephus, who changed sides and joined the Roman army. He includes this passage in his autobiography:

> And when I was sent by Titus Caesar with Caerealius, and a thousand horsemen, to a certain village called Thecoa, in order to know whether it were a place fit for a camp, as I came back, I saw many captives crucified, and remembered three of them as my former acquaintance. I was very sorry at this in my mind, and went with tears in my eyes to Titus, and told him of them; so he immediately commanded them to be taken down, and to have the greatest care taken of them in order to their recovery; yet two of them died under the physician's hands, while the third recovered. [IV:75]

It is not clear how long the survivor spent on the cross, but a considerable time is implied. And the time factor is very important.

One of the main investigators of crucifixion and the way in which the victims died was Dr Pierre Barbet, a French surgeon and anatomist. From the publication of Enrie's photographs in 1931 onwards, he made a close study of the wounds on the Shroud, with particular emphasis on the details of crucifixion.

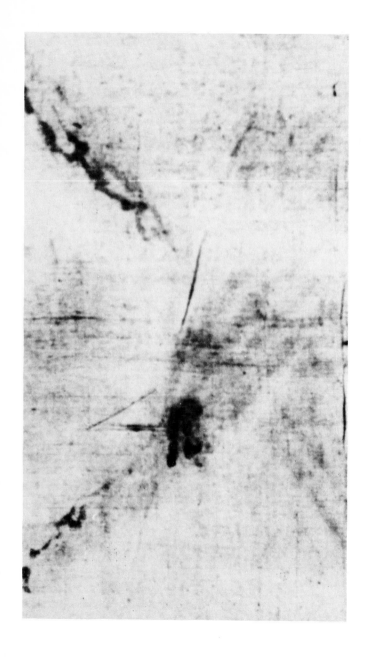

The hand area on the Shroud image.

In his medical post he was able to experiment with cadavers, and this meant that where Vignon had reasoned, Barbet was able to perform practical experiments, sometimes with surprising results.

Considering the nail wound in the wrist first, Vignon had presumed that nails in the palms would not support a body on a plain cross. Barbet proved it using a dead body. Vignon pointed out that the nail had apparently been driven through the wrist, and realized that this would have given sufficient strength to hold the body. Barbet actually drove a nail through the wrist of an amputed arm. The wrist is a mass of bones, and it was not until he placed the nail against it, and struck hard with the hammer, the nail forced its way through an unsuspected gap called 'The Space of Destot'. As the nail went through, it penetrated or displaced the long tendon, coming from the forearm, that flexes the thumb, which was drawn across the palm.[1] When he examined the Shroud and found that on neither hand was the thumb represented, he felt sure he had found the reason, and because any painter would have painted them in, he had discovered another potent indication that the stains were not forged. In fact the thumbs might also be missing because they were tucked under the opposite palms naturally, but the argument against the likelihood of the cloth being painted still holds.

The next question to be investigated was the exact cause of death. When the victim was raised on the cross, assuming it was the normal sort, the plain *crux immissa* seen on Christian altars, his body would have sagged and his weight been borne on his arms. Barbet fastened volunteers on crosses, binding their hands and feet to the wood, to observe what happened. Each volunteer found that his chest was kept fully expanded when his weight was borne by his arms, with no possibility of exhaling. In this position he was slowly suffocated, and cramps which began in the arms spread to the trunk and legs. Because he could not breathe out and then in, the oxygen in his blood decreased and he would have asphyxiated in a matter of minutes. The only way the volunteer could stay alive was to press up with his feet, lessening the strain on his hands and arms, and breathing out and in rapidly until he had to collapse again through exhaustion. Eventually, and after a fairly short time, tiredness prevented the volunteer from pressing up on his feet, and he would have died from asphyxiation if not released.[2]

Barbet used the two positions to explain the V-shaped blood-marks on the left wrist. Although emerging from one wound, there are two quite separate streams of blood. Using pencil and paper instead of a live body, Barbet sketched the angles of the arms in the two positions, the one when all the weight was on the arms and the one when the feet had pressed the body up to allow breathing out and in. Measuring the two angles made by the V-shaped blood-marks with the line of the forearm, he constructed theoretically the two positions of the body so that those lines would have been vertical in the two positions. It seemed very plausible, and has apparently remained unquestioned until now.

There is one obvious problem with this idea. The victim must have switched from one position to the other quite frequently, so that the branches of the bloodstains would not have been distinct lines. There would at least have been a zigzagging between the two directions. To have them separate, the arm must have been in one position for some time while the blood slowly ran down to the end of the first trickle, and then for a similar period in the second position.

The question of time is vital. It must have been extremely difficult, with the feet nailed against the vertical beam, and the knees bent, to have pressed up sufficiently to exhale once or twice, and to have held that position must have been very painful. So little breathing would have been possible that it is difficult to imagine a victim could have stayed alive for more than a few minutes.

There are few ancient records of crucifixion, but those that do exist indicate how long it took for the unfortunate victims to die. It was certainly not quick. The slowness was part of the torture, as well as the humiliation, hunger, thirst and exhaustion. Passers-by were meant to learn from the examples made of the victims, which is why crucifixions took place outside city walls and beside main roads. After defeating Spartacus, Crassus had six thousand prisoners nailed to crosses beside the Via Appia between Capua and Rome,[3] and Titus had up to five hundred prisoners a day nailed up on crosses outside the walls of Jerusalem, hoping the gruesome sight of countless crosses would persuade the besieged to surrender.[4] As for the slowness of the death, Seneca, in Epistle 101 to Lucilius, writes that a lengthy process of dying is no longer worthy of the name of 'life', and follows it with a description of the gradual death of a victim of crucifixion:

> Can anyone be found who would prefer wasting away in pain dying limb by limb, or letting out his life drop by drop, rather than expiring once for all? Can any man be found willing to be fastened to the accursed tree, long sickly, already deformed, swelling with ugly weals on shoulders and chest, and drawing the breath of life amid long-drawn-out agony? He would have many excuses for dying even before mounting the cross.[5]

The New Bible Dictionary says of crucifixion: 'Death by this method was usually quite protracted, rarely supervening before thirty-six hours, and on occasion taking as long as nine days.'[6]

Ancient Jewish writings also indicate that death by crucifixion took a long time. The rabbis, in the Mishna, entered into long discussions as to how death was defined; it was not sufficient merely to see a man crucified on a cross, unless animals had eaten his body. In the Jerusalem Talmud, they point out that a rich lady might redeem a victim's body, the implication being that rich ladies would bribe officials to take down the sufferers and that in some cases at least they recovered. The rabbis also accepted that a man being crucified could authorize a by-stander to issue a bill of divorcement to his wife, so that crucifixion victims were clearly regarded as being of sound enough mind to be able to conduct legal business.

These accounts do not fit in with the very brief, excruciating agonies suggested by the experiments of Barbet. Similar research was conducted by Dr Hermann Moedder, a German radiologist. He experimented by tying up on plain crosses university students – volunteers of course! He found that they fainted after 6–12 minutes because their blood pressure dropped, and that death would have followed in under half an hour. Again, there was no question of being sane enough to carry out legal business from the cross, and death would have come much earlier than records suggest. However, Moedder found that if the legs were supported every three minutes, normal circulation returned. He concluded that if the victim had had a foot-rest, he could have survived for hours, even days.[7] His reason for choosing a foot-rest instead of the *sedile* of historical records was the fact that the way of finally despatching victims was by breaking their legs. He reasoned that this act would not have killed them had they been sitting on a *sedile*. That is true. However, they were possibly tipped forward off their supports when the time came to finish them off, and their legs would have been broken to prevent their pressing themselves up onto their seats again.

A useful reference book on crucifixion is called exactly that, *Crucifixion,* in the English translation. It is by Martin Hengel, and in the original German had the lengthy title, *Mors turpissima crucis: Die Kreuzigung in der antiken Weld und die 'Torheit' des 'Wortes vom Kreuz'*. Hengel outlines the wide variety of practice, summarizing it thus:

> Even in the Roman empire, where there might be said to be some kind of 'norm' for the course of the execution (it included a flogging beforehand, and the victim often carried the beam to the place of execution, where he was nailed to it with outstretched arms, raised up and seated on a small wooden peg), the form of execution could vary considerably: crucifixion was a punishment in which the caprice and sadism of the executioners were given full rein.

From this it is clear that although there was wide variation, the normal support for the victim was not a footrest, the support represented in medieval paintings and used by Dr Moedder, but the projecting peg, the *sedile*, astride which the victim usually sat. Seneca, in his *Epistolae*, speaks of sitting on the cross, and implies that the projection had a sharp edge for the additional discomfort of the sufferer. St Justin describes the peg as 'this wood of the cross which is fixed in the middle, which stick upwards like a horn, on which those who are crucified are seated'. St Irenaeus says that the cross had five extremities; it is on the fifth that the crucified man rests.

The alternative support for prolonging the agony was the *suppedaneum,* a horizontal bracket coming out from the upright to which the feet were nailed. Although the foot-rest was always selected as the support when artists began painting crucifixion scenes, the first references to it in writings do not appear until much later than the *sedile*; not until the sixth century, in fact, in *De Gloria Martyrii* by Gregory of Tours.[8]

It is worth studying the stains on the cloth to see whether there is an indication which kind of support, if any, the man in the Shroud had. It is highly likely he had one, if he did not die but slipped into a coma.

The most indicative stains are the blood-marks on the wrist and forearms. On the left wrist, the only one visible, are the V-shaped blood-marks, at an angle to the arm, while further up the left forearm most of the marks are approximately parallel to one branch of the V. On the right forearm the blood-marks run parallel to the forearm, the right wrist being hidden. They are quite different from the left arm, and the right forearm must have been vertical a long time for the blood to trickle all the way down it from the wound on the wrist.

I carried out an experiment at Trent Polytechnic to investigate the significance of these marks. Blood-marks similar to the ones in the Shroud were painted on a volunteer's wrists and arms. This was done by projecting a slide on him while matching red marks were applied. A cross was then constructed with scaffolding in the Drama Studio. Hanging from the cross-beam with his hands equidistant from the vertical, facing the cross so that the blood-marks could be seen, the volunteer tried to pull himself up with his right forearm vertical so that the blood could have flowed down it through gravity. His left arm was nearly horizontal then, and his right biceps were under a very great strain, since his right arm was supporting almost his

The conscious and the unconscious positions on the Cross (with the volunteer facing it).

entire weight. It seemed entirely unrealistic that the crucified man would have pulled himself up to this extraordinary, asymmetric position to exhale, especially considering the force on his right nail-wound, and he could not possibly have held it while the blood slowly trickled down his arm.

Next, a short piece was attached to the upright for him to sit on. It was simple to adjust it to the right height so that he could sit on it symmetrically, the marks across the left forearm and one limb of the V on his left wrist being vertical. This would have been the normal position when conscious. He was then asked to relax, as if losing consciousness, and topple to the right. Not only were the stains on his right forearm then vertical, but the second arm of the V was as well. He also found this position natural and comfortable.

The chest wound provides additional evidence that there must have been a *sedile*. A sharp instrument pierced the chest just under the right armpit, higher than in the position in the Shroud for the skin would have moved as the arm was raised. If his body had been symmetrical when this wound was made, the blood would have dripped down his stomach and right leg, and the marks of it would have been visible along the cloth. This is not the case, and none can be seen below the chest. If the man was stabbed in the unconscious position on the *sedile*, the blood would have flowed down his side and so would not have been shown on the cloth. When he was placed in the cloth after being brought down to the ground, the blood flow round his back on the dorsal image was clearly much more watery than the other blood-marks. This is not surprising. When he was scourged, he would probably have had a pleural effusion, a watery liquid between his lungs and his rib-cage. Collapsed unconscious to the right, this would have been drained when the chest was pierced, so that watery liquid as well as blood would have come out.

All this provides more strong evidence for the Shroud's being genuine. There are very many paintings of crucifixion, for this is what happened to the historical character known as Jesus Christ, but if they show a support for the body at all, they show a foot-rest. If the Shroud was painted, it would probably be the only medieval painting indicating the use of a *sedile* in a crucifixion.

The blood-marks indicate clearly that the man had a cross with a *sedile* on which he sat. There are some other things about him revealed by the stains.

References

1. Barton, N. J., 'Without Thumbs . . . a Theory', *General Report and Proceedings of the British Society for the Turin Shroud*, Autumn 1979.
2. Humber, T., *The Fifth Gospel*, Pocket Books, 1974, p. 125.
3. Hengel, M., *Crucifixion*, S.C.M., 1977, p. 155.
4. Ibid., p. 26.
5. Ibid., p. 30.
6. *New Bible Dictionary*, Inter Varsity Fellowship, 1962, p. 282.
7. Willis, D., 'Did He Die on the Cross?', *The Ampleforth Journal*, 74 (1969), p. 33.
8. Barbet, P., *A Doctor at Calvary*, Image Books, 1963, p. 43.

Seven
DETAILED OBSERVATIONS

The presence of a *sedile* on the cross of the man in the Shroud means that all the research into how men died when crucified on plain crosses is irrelevant in his case. It would have been possible for him to have been on the cross for a day or days, and then fallen into a coma before being taken down and placed in the cloth. The V-shaped blood-marks on his wrist suggest that he was suspended a considerable time in the conscious position, and then a similar time slumped to the right while the blood trickled down the second limb of the V. His heart must have been beating throughout to keep up the blood presure from the wound.

When the nail or nails were removed from his feet and he was taken down from the cross, blood flowed towards his heels from the nail-holes. This is not conclusive proof that his heart was still beating. When a dead body is moved, blood can flow out of wounds by gravity. However, the quantity of it under and beside his feet, and round his back, would suggest that he was in a coma rather than having been dead for some time.

There are some further details about the man to be learnt from the stains, and the fact that his body was placed in a long stretch of rich material also needs exploring.

Firstly, his stature. Clearly, looking at his image, he was

well proportioned, and it might be presumed that close measurement of his physique should be possible. Unfortunately, precision is difficult on two counts: the edges of his body merge into the background, and the depth of the folding of the cloth into hollows has to be guessed. For these reasons the estimates of his height have varied between five foot four inches and six feet.[1] Measurements of the lengths of the images on the flat cloth have given 6.7257 feet for the front image and 6.8596 feet for the back,[2] although such accuracy is fanciful considering the blurred edges. The height most commonly estimated for the man is about five feet eleven inches, which would have been tall for the Mediterranean peoples, but not excessively so.[3]

It would help to know where the man lived to judge what race he belonged to, and the fact that he was crucified helps here. Crucifixion itself had many forms, from a simple nailing to a stake to the man being fixed upside down on a cross shaped like an X. Sometimes the victim was alive, sometimes it was his dead body that was nailed up for display. From the Persians it spread among many barbarian races, and was taken over by the Romans, though not for Roman citizens. Constantine banned it throughout the Roman Empire in about AD 341,[4] so that the man in the cloth would have suffered his fate before that.

The area in which the cloth was made would then have been the eastern provinces of the Roman Empire. This narrows down his race. His looks are important, for the Romans and Greeks in the Empire shaved and dressed their hair, but the orthodox Jews left it to grow, except perhaps when mourning, wearing it at the back as a pigtail. The signs on the dorsal image of an unbound pigtail are also indicative.[5] So he was probably a Jew, although it is nowhere near conclusive at this stage. In view of investigations in a later chapter, references will be made to Jewish customs when discussing the Shroud and its marks.

The stains suggest what sort of environment the body was in when lying in the cloth. The image of the face seems unnaturally thin, and the cloth does not fall round the sides of the body as would be expected if it had been lain on a flat surface. Also the back image folds up round the sides to give the same width as the front, which would not occur on a surface that was hard as well as flat. Paul Vignon, in considering the narrowness of the image of the face, pictured the cloth held up by cushions or similar supports at the sides of the head and holding up the hair. This seems credible, but supports would have been necessary all down the sides of the body as well. This does not adequately explain the back image.

A more likely explanation of the top surface is that the space in which the body lay had a rim round it, so that the top of the cloth went directly from the body to the rim, keeping the top image narrow. The exact kind of space is uncertain, but either a trough or a sarcophagus would have given the right effect. It would have to be about as tall as the height of a prone body, perhaps a foot, so that the cloth could have hung across to its top edge. The width of the space could not have been much wider than the body, for the weight of the cloth would have dragged it back, so it can be thought of as being similar to a tight-fitting coffin. There is confirmatory evidence of this in the hands and arms. If a person lies on the floor and folds his hands in the 'fig-leaf' position as in the Shroud, he finds that if he goes limp his elbows will fall to the ground and his hands come apart. So the elbows must have been prevented from falling to the sides of the body by the constraints of the space, the sides of the trough or coffin.

This still does not answer the problem of the width of the back image. The cloth is only 43 inches wide. If the middle 20 inches pressed against the back, this would have left less than a foot on either side, too little to stretch up to be supported on the rim. The edges of the cloth must therefore have laid along the edges of the body. Some other explanation is required for the broad image of the back. On the VP-8 Image Analyser the man's back had no subtle slopes but appeared uniformly flat, as if the skin had been evenly in contact with the cloth over the whole area. This could not happen with a hard surface.

The answer is probably that the body rested on sand. This was apparently normal practice in areas of the Middle East, and is mentioned in the Mishna.[6] The cross section of the body and the cloth in the open coffin or trough would have been as shown in the diagram below.

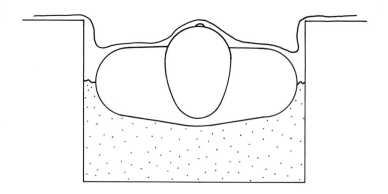

Note that the arms would have been kept well above the sand, and this would be confirmed if no arms appear on the dorsal image on the cloth. Unfortunately, these crucial areas are obscured by the broadest scorch stains and the widest patches on the the whole Shroud.

Some other points can be deduced by applying the thermographic hypothesis, with the darkness of the body-marks depending on the temperature of the cloth, to particular areas. The surprising darkness round the nose can be explained by the minimal exhaling of warm breath. The nose projects so far from the face that the cloth must have been held away from the skin all round it; but the moustache and beard are stained, as well as the skin on the sides of the face.

When considering the temperature of the cloth, the darkness of the hair, as well as the beard and moustache, is difficult to understand. They would have been considerably colder than the body. Perhaps it is because there are two factors to the darkness of the stain: the temperature and the concentration of the developing agent. The developing agent

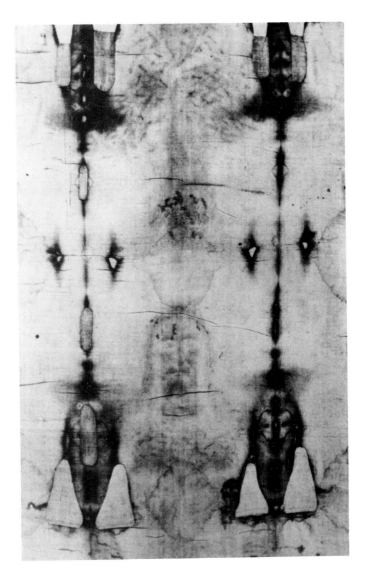

Photograph showing how the stains caused by the back of the head are wider than the face on the front.

– ammonia, if Vignon was correct – could have been much more prevalent in the hair than on the surface of the skin. But this is no more than a vague guess at the moment.

The darkness of the stains underneath the feet indicate, as Vignon surmised, that there must have been material underneath the feet pressing the bottom of the cloth against the soles. The stains all the way down the backs of the legs show that the knees were not bent, so the soles must have come up at a considerable angle to the horizontal, and the cloth would not have touched them at all unless it was pressed against them by a pile of material. At the other end of the body, the blood-marks and body-marks all round the back of the hair show there must have been material around and under the head as well, in the form of a pillow. This is more likely than simply rolls of material by the side of the head, as Vignon suggested, for two reasons. Firstly, all round the back of the head was in contact with the cloth. Secondly, there is evidence that the head was pressed up: the back of the neck looks as if it was stretched, and the dorsal image on the Shroud is longer than the frontal.[7]

There is little more that has been deduced about the man, his ordeal, and his position when in the cloth.

It is relevant to consider how he came to be placed naked, and unwashed, in an expensive length of cloth, for a considerable time. Contemporary customs and beliefs matter in this respect.

If the man was a Jew, his body would have been considered as cursed to his fellow Jews. In Deuteronomy (21:23), part of the Torah or sacred Mosaic Law, it says quite specifically that 'he that is hanged (upon the tree) is accursed of God'. They considered *any* dead body polluting to the touch,[8] and this would have applied much more strongly to someone dying in this way.

This is why the rich cloth, and the body presumably placed in it somewhere with a steady temperature like a tomb or cellar, come as a surprise. Normally the Romans would have been responsible for the bodies of those crucified. Often they were left up for the animals to devour. Probably many were thrown into a communal grave or limepit. The man in the cloth avoided these fates, but he was also not given the proper burial rites.

It is not possible to be certain about Jewish burial customs as long ago as the times when crucifixions were carried out, but there are probabilities that can be deduced from studying the few descriptions preserved in the Rabbinic literature. Firstly, the eyes were closed, and the chin may have been bound up at this stage.[9] The corpse was then washed with warm, perfumed water and anointed with an unguent perhaps consisting mainly of salt, honey, myrrh and cedar oil,[10] but it is not known whether the anointing was done by pouring a fluid on the body, sprinkling the clothes before putting them on, rubbing the body or immersing it.

Next, it was clothed in its burial garments. It was thought a dishonour for a corpse to be naked, and grave-clothes became finer and more expensive as time went on, so much so that dying people were often abandoned by their relatives so that the community would be responsible for the expense of the funeral.[11] At last Rabbi Gamaliel, who died in AD 57-58, directed that he should be buried in the simplest of linen garments, and his example was eagerly followed. Whatever clothes were put on the body, the face was left uncovered. The hands and feet were probably bound, and the jaw tied up with a band.

There was probably one exception to this rule of washing and anointing corpses, although the Jewish literature describing it – the 16th century *Code of Jewish Law* – dates from well after the end of crucifixion. Blood was considered so important to the Jews that if a man died a violent death, and his blood was spilt onto his clothes, they were not removed and he was buried unwashed. This could possibly have applied in very early times as well. However the man in the Shroud was naked, and although he would not have been washed because of the blood on his skin if this applied, completely wrapping him so that his face as well as his body was covered seems surprising. It is likely that the use of the Shroud implies a hurried and provisional covering of the body.

The reason for the anointing, and placing the body on sand, was to put off the beginning of corruption for as long as possible, three days at least. The Jews and many other races believed the soul remained with the body for three days after death and might re-enter it during that period, allowing the body to come alive again. The period of mourning was seven days, but for the first three, relatives kept visiting the tomb in case the body recovered from death; during this period the tomb was not properly closed. Families sometimes hired men to watch by the dead for them.

The existence of these beliefs suggests that mistakes were commonly made, bodies being interred in what is now known as a deep coma. In view of the means by which death was recognized then, this is not surprising. To people at this time life resided as breath in the chest; when a body showed no signs of breathing, particularly if the chest was wounded, it was declared dead. The Greek word *pneuma* could mean breath or life, spirit or ghost, so the phrase 'he gave up the ghost' or 'he yielded up his spirit' could be just as well translated 'he stopped breathing'. The functions of the heart, and the circulation of the blood, were not discovered for more than a millennium and a half. Even today, with all our sophisticated medical knowledge, people recover after being declared clinically dead, sometimes in the mortuary.

It has been argued that the Romans, being experienced in killing by crucifixion, could not possibly have made a mistake and allowed the body of someone who was only comatose to be taken away. The Roman centurion in charge had the duty, as *exactor mortis,* of confirming death in the victims. The answer is that the man in the cloth *was* absolutely dead by the centurion's standards and experience. If men before him, after choking on offered wine for instance, had slumped to the side in what is now known as a coma, they would not have survived, for being dumped in a limepit or communal grave would have given no chance of recovery. The centurion would not have known that full life could return from such a condition. The circumstances of the man in the cloth were probably unique.

Up to this point the book has been a brief survey showing how far the study of the cloth and its stains, and the relevant historical sources, can take us at the moment.

Many of the questions raised have not been answered: questions such as why the crucified man was placed, naked and unwashed, in a rich length of cloth. What happened to his body then? And what could have caused those strange blood-marks in the skin round the top of his head? In the absence of further evidence it would be almost impossible to think of *any* reasonable answers to such questions. If we knew *who* he was, that might help, provided the historical records of the man's death were fairly detailed.

Now some people have claimed that the stains on this particular cloth were made by the body of the man known to history as Jesus Christ. This means that the information in the written records of his life should be examined to see if there is any possibility of this coincidence.

As Jesus was the founder of the religion of Christianity, the possibility of objective, unemotional judgement being applied to the further search is much less likely. Before continuing with the quest, it is worth summarizing the conclusions derived from the straightforward scientific analysis of the cloth and its stains.

References

1. Rinaldi, P. M., *The Man in the Shroud,* Futura, 1974, p. 84.
2. Humber, T., *The Fifth Gospel,* Pocket Books, 1974, p. 29.
3. Wilson, I., *The Turin Shroud,* Gollancz, 1978, p. 21.
4. Humber, T., op. cit., p. 43.
5. Wilson, I., op. cit., p. 32.
6. Robinson, J. A. T., 'The Shroud and the New Testament', *Face to Face with the Turin Shroud,* Mayhew, McCrimmon and A. R. Mowbray, 1978, p. 71.
7. Humber T., op. cit., p. 29.
8. Ibid., p. 52.
9. O'Rahilly, A., *The Burial of Christ,* Cork University Press, 1942, p. 1.
10. Ibid., p. 6.
11. Humber, T., op. cit., p. 53.
12. O'Rahilly, A., op. cit, p. 13.

SUMMARY OF
PART ONE

1. The large twill piece of cloth, 14'3" by 3'7", is a good quality three-to-one twill weave in pure linen with only the odd traces of cotton as impurities.

2. The evidence of the fabric, and pollen on its surface, indicates manufacture in the Middle East – Syria or Palestine rather than Egypt.

3. The date of manufacture is uncertain. The technology existed three or four thousand years ago, but equivalent *linen* cloths did not appear regularly until the end of the Middle Ages.

4. Very dim stains and patches can be seen on the cloth. The main marks were the result of damage from a fire in 1532.

5. Between the scorch marks can be seen the faint images of the front and back of a man's body.

6. These images could not have been painted, nor forged by any other known method.

7. The man has wounds from scourging, crucifixion and a stab-wound in the chest. He also has blood-marks from where the skin round the top of his head was punctured.

8. The blood-marks were caused by human blood, of group AB. The formation of the body-stains is not yet understood.

9. He was crucified on a cross with a *sedile* on which he sat upright for some hours. He then toppled to the right, presumably on losing consciousness, to remain in that second position for a similarly long time.

10. While toppled to the right, he was stabbed in the right side of his chest just below the armpit. The watery trickle of blood from the wound suggests that he was sufering from a pleural effusion as a result of being scourged.

11. He was still in a coma when he was placed in the cloth and must have remained in it for a long time while the stains developed.

12. His body was in the cloth in an open coffin or trough-shaped space, in the bottom of which was sand. Some soft material was under his shrouded head pillowing it, while another pile of material was beneath his feet, holding the cloth against his soles.

13. His body was not prepared for burial. It was unwashed and unanointed, and was naked under the cloth.

14. As he was in a deep coma, although absolutely dead by contemporary standards, he could have recovered at any time within a few days, or died.

15. His body left the cloth alive or newly dead, since decay did not affect the image.

Part Two

THE
MAN

Eight

THE WRITTEN EVIDENCE

Christianity has more nominal adherents than any other religion, and one might expect the life of its founder to have blazed brilliantly in the records of the times in which he lived. In fact, if we ignore the literature of the Church he founded, he is barely mentioned, and the odd record that does appear may well have been inserted or altered by copyists who were his followers.

It is true that he spent almost all his life in Galilee, a remote and obscure part of the Roman Empire, probably as a humble manual worker. Nevertheless, the last part of his life was momentous, and he is believed to have been crucified, buried, and then to have come to life again. The witnesses to this became the firm foundation of a movement that affected the whole of the known world. For this reason, the fact that no account of his life was given by the Jewish historian Josephus seems surprising. John the Baptist was mentioned by Josephus, who should also have had evidence of the strength of the followers of Jesus. Apart from Josephus, Plutarch and Tacitus were historians of the generation after Jesus, and their silence is also unexpected at first sight.

In view of the way Christianity shaped the course of history, so that the years have been measured from the estimated date of birth of Jesus, it is hard to appreciate that the life of this man did not seem all that important at the time. There were plenty of others like him who made claims, spoke wise thoughts, and worked remarkable cures. It was his crucifixion, death and recovery from death that supplied the spark that lit the fire. And once lit it took time to reach red heat. The beginnings of all religions are very localized. Perhaps some prophet in Africa or guru in India is dying even now who will alter the future as fundamentally as Jesus did; yet all but a few will not have heard of him, and the same may be true of the next generation, in spite of the rapidity of modern communications.

But accounts of the life of Jesus do exist in the Gospels, and in this Christianity is fortunate. With many religions the life of the founder was not compiled from documents until a very long time after his death, and then in a disjointed form.[1] But how reliable those accounts are as records of the life of Jesus must first be established.

The first point is that the Gospels were not written as histories, or biographies. They were compilations of the traditions of the Church written down for edification, worship, discipline and defence. They were not composed until decades after the events they describe, and were anonymous, being designated as gospels 'according to . . .' in the second century. Their principal authors were probably not original disciples of Jesus, although John's Gospel may include recollections by St John himself, and likewise Matthew's Gospel may possibly contain a small amount of material from the disciple of that name. St Mark is believed to have been inspired by St Peter.

The passage of a very long time before the writing down began is unfortunate, for time can warp memories as well as cut into them. There are several likely reasons for this hiatus. The first Christians were not an educated group, and this comes out in the biblical Greek in which the Gospels were composed, which has the strictly limited vocabulary of the common man.[2] The cost of materials must have mattered as well. But, most important, the early Church expected Jesus to return to earth in glory very shortly and establish 'the end of all things'. In such circumstances it must have appeared a waste of time to write down records for succeeding generations. Lastly, the tradition for the oral transmission of teaching was so strong, and memories so well trained, that there was not felt to be the same need to have a written record.[3]

The need came. The second coming of Jesus did not happen as expected, and disciples died who had hoped to witness it. The spread of the Church, the interest of the new converts in the life of the founder, the differences with Jews and Roman authorities, and several other reasons, stimulated the desire for written records. The first Gospel, Mark's, was compiled soon after the death of St Peter, and that was probably 35 years or more after the Crucifixion. Mark's Gospel was followed by Matthew's and Luke's, and since both these authors used Mark's Gospel as a major source, they view events from a similar viewpoint: hence the three are called the Synoptic Gospels.

The question arises, if the Gospels were not written down for at least thirty years, how much confidence may be placed in them as historical records?

It depends what is being studied. Consider the teaching of Jesus they contain. Memorization of whole books was quite normal before writing was cheap and convenient. To assist it, teaching was carefully framed, with words selected like musical notes so that the rhythm could be remembered.[4] The sayings of Jesus in some cases turn out to be in verse when translated back into Aramaic,[5] and besides this technique repetition, and the use of parables, ensured that his message was preserved accurately. It is also quite possible that at a very early stage a collection of the sayings of Jesus was assembled and written down to act as a source book and reminder for teachers.[6] The teaching, therefore, is probably very accurately recorded, although it may have been adapted slightly for the readerships for which the Gospels were written.

Some of the details of time and place did suffer distortion, however, and this can be seen from the way the Gospels differ. In the most extreme example, the cleansing of the Temple occurs at the beginning of the Ministry in John, and at the end in the Synoptics.

There are other indications of distortion. When Matthew's

and Luke's elaborations are compared with the originals in Mark's Gospel, the way they altered the stories for the particular communities they were addressing themselves to is obvious. A natural desire to exaggerate is plain, so that analysts trying to seek the truth have as one of their techniques to accept the least sensational account. Sometimes the changes seem pointless. For instance, the title on the Cross is different in all four accounts.

So far only the Synoptic Gospels have been considered. The fourth, John's, is quite different. This is not just an account of the life, preaching and sayings of Jesus. It is more a theological interpretation, by the author, of these aspects. The other Gospels were probably already in circulation, but the author of the Fourth Gospel did not necessarily draw on these. What he did was to tell the story of a character, rather as a modern historical novelist does, interpreting it in terms of the philosophy and theology of the end of the first century.[7]

In John's Gospel Jesus says quite different things in a quite different language, and the turns of speech, the parables of the Kingdom, the Aramaic verse-forms, and the talk of the Son of Man are largely replaced by exalted mystic communications from a heavenly Lord.[8] Many of the stories may well be sheer invention, to provide symbolic proofs of the Messiahship of Jesus. The wedding at Cana and the raising of Lazarus are two of them, being the first and last of the seven signs. To see the extent of his inventive powers, the raising of Lazarus would have been John's adaptation of the story which became the rich man and Lazarus in Luke. If Jesus had raised Lazarus from the dead as described by John, the incident would certainly have been reported in the other Gospels. For these reasons John's Gospel would seem the least reliable historically. Indeed, at one stage critics considered it to be valueless in this regard compared with the Synoptics, but more recently, particularly since the work of Professor Dodd in Cambridge, a less harsh view has prevailed.

Few points have caused more arguments than the authorship of the Fourth Gospel. A central argument is whether there was a single author or more than one. The material indicates there could have been three separate sources: the Witness, who was perhaps John the Apostle; the Evangelist, who was the main author of the work, and the Redactor, who finally revised its order and added a few passages.[9] But arguing against this is the style of writing, which is uniform and suggests a single author. The title of the Gospel assigns it to St John, but this is now considered unlikely for various reasons, principally an early statement by a second-century bishop (Papias, quoted by Eusebius) that it was written by one of St John's disciples, John the Presbyter or the Elder, under the direction of the apostle. A minor reason is that his description of himself as 'the disciple whom Jesus loved' would have been most immodest.

For the study of the Shroud it does not matter a great deal whether there was one or more than one author. The crucial point is that there is strong evidence with regard to this particular Gospel that the descriptions of the Crucifixion and the tomb in which the body of Jesus was placed may have been written down by an eye-witness, or by someone with whom the eye-witness communicated. There is thus a much closer relationship with the original event than in the Synoptic Gospels.

To summarize, St John's Gospel as a whole is much the least reliable historically, particularly as far as the teaching of Jesus is concerned. The author has embellished and interpreted to such an extent that it is difficult to distinguish between what Jesus said and did and what the author thinks Jesus should have said and did. Nevertheless, among the sands of the discourses, the signs and the conversations, glisten the jewels from the memory of the eye-witness, probably St John the Apostle.

The other three gospels are much more straightforward. In them the main outline of Jesus' teaching is clear, and their writers do not clutter up the text with their own interpretations. But the distance to the source of each item of historical observation, the number of mouths in the train of communication, is usually impossible to determine. Some matter may be only second-hand, the author writing down what the participant saw or heard, though it is difficult to classify much in this way. An example is the story of Peter's denial, which must be true, and possibly was told to Mark by St Peter himself.

With John's Gospel the fragments that come within this category may be recognized because they include the phrase 'the disciple whom Jesus loved', and where those words occur there are also surprising little details, touches etched into the memory of the original eye-witness, proclaiming their authenticity. The beginning of the account of the Last Supper (John 13: 2-30), the Crucifixion (19: 23-37), and the discovery of the empty tomb (20: 1-9) all have the beloved disciple present, and although the words of Jesus contained in the passages show signs of the interpretation of the Evangelist rather than the memory of the Witness, the visual descriptions are remarkably powerful. Less reliable for textual reasons is the final scene by the lake in Galilee (21: 1-25), but that may be the eye-witness again. The clarity of image in the description of the High Priest's courtyard (18: 12-27) suggests that perhaps he was also 'the other disciple' with St Peter on that occasion.

The great worth of the testimony of the original eye-witness is emphasized in the text very strongly at one place, and it is a place that is remarkably relevant to the study of the cloth. Remember that the victim in the Shroud was stabbed under the right armpit while in the unconscious position, clearly to make sure he was dead. His legs were not broken. Thorough searches by Vignon in 1939 and Wuenschel in 1953 found only one report of victims being stabbed during their crucifixion, apart from St John's Gospel. In about AD 290 Marcellus and Marcellinus were despatched with a spear because their constant praise of God annoyed the sentries.[10] So the victim in the Shroud was very rare in this respect. Remember, too that the blood-stains from the wound, which flowed in a watery trickle round the back, suggest that he had water fluid between his lungs and rib-cage, a pleural effusion caused by the scourging. Compare these points with the description of the eye-witness in John's Gospel:

> But when they came to Jesus, they found that he was already dead, so they did not break his legs. But one of the soldiers

stabbed his side with a lance, and at once there was a flow of blood and water. This is vouched for by an eye-witness, whose evidence is to be trusted. He knows that he speaks the truth, so that you too may believe [19: 33-36].

The coincidence is extraordinary. Perhaps it *is* just possible that the man whose body left marks in the Shroud was indeed this unique historical character, Jesus Christ. A full comparison must be made between what the Shroud tells of the man it contained and the written accounts of the Crucifixion of Jesus, keeping as far as possible to the account of the eye-witness in John's Gospel, in preference to the Synoptics.

References

1. Grant, F. C., *The Gospels – Their Origin and Growth,* Faber and Faber, 1965, p. 25.
2. Leon-Dufour, X., *The Gospels and the Jesus of History,* Collins, 1968, p. 74.
3. Grant, F. C., op. cit., pp. 26, 29.
4. Gerhardsson, B., *The Origins of the Gospel Traditions,* S.C.M., 1979, p. 19.
5. Cupitt, D., and P. Armstrong, *Who Was Jesus?* B.B.C., 1977, p. 53.
6. Dodd, C. H., *The Founder of Christianity,* Collins, 1972, p. 20.
7. Guy, R. A., *The Study of the Gospels,* Macmillan, 1967, p. 43.
8. Cupitt, D., and P. Armstrong, op. cit., p. 56.
9. Grant, F. C., op. cit., p. 176.
10. Meacham, W., 'The Authentication of the Turin Shroud: An Issue in Archaeological Epistemology', *Current Archaeology,* Vol. 24, No. 3, June 1983, p. 292.

Nine

MAKING COMPARISONS

The stains on the cloth reveal in considerable detail the physique of the man once contained in the Shroud, as well as the ordeals he suffered and the way in which he lay while the stains developed. The Gospel accounts must be studied to see whether the details of Jesus match.

Beginning with the man in the cloth, the facts of his having been scourged and crucified and the probability of his Jewish origins do not make him particularly unusual. Thousands of tragic candidates fulfilled those conditions. As was pointed out at the end of the last chapter, the stab wound in the chest has much more significance, for written records suggest that crucifixion victims were normally put out of their agony by having their legs broken. Since it was normal to have a *sedile* on the cross, this method of giving the *coup de grace,* the *crurifragium,* was administered so that the victim could not push himself up onto the *sedile* again. We know that the two men who were crucified with Jesus suffered this; and the lower leg-bones of the only crucified Jew so far unearthed – found in an ossuary in a tomb in Jerusalem in 1968 – were severely fractured. The written accounts are too few, however, for this to be regarded as conclusive.

Much more important are the blood-marks round the top of the head. Putting aside for a moment the Gospel story of

Jesus, there is no recorded torture instrument that could have produced such marks. Lacking knowledge of the crown of thorns, mentioned in the Gospels as having been placed on the head of Jesus, it would be extremely difficult to think of anything that could have caused those marks. It is the connection between this aspect of the torture of Jesus and those particular marks on the Shroud that gives the strongest indication that it wrapped his body.

There were other points to be deduced about the man in the Shroud from the stains. He was crucified on a cross with a *sedile,* on which he sat upright for some hours before toppling to the right, unconscious, for another considerable length of time. On traditional Christian representations of the Cross there is no such projection. This difference is important, but it is clear from early Christian writings that the exact form of cross used in Jesus's case was not described or known, and for one good reason: the cross was a symbol of shame and humiliation to the Jews, because of the pronouncement of Deuteronomy (21: 23). This is why, although thousands of Jews were crucified by the Romans, the cross never became a symbol of Jewish suffering,[1] and the idea of a crucified Messiah was particularly offensive.

There was, therefore, a good reason why the Jews did not pass on a precise description of the cross used in Jesus' case, and the same apparently applied to the Gentile Church. Paul found his preaching of the cross 'a stumbling-block' (Galatians 5:11). Not until long after the Emperor Constantine substituted hanging as the state penalty could Christians, by then predominantly Gentile, bring themselves to portray the crucifixion itself in their art,[2] but by then even the form of the cross was uncertain. They knew from the Gospels that the cross bar was carried by Jesus and a bystander, which ruled out one shaped like an X. The fact that a title was fixed to it, suggested that a *crux immissa,* as on Christian altars, was used rather than one shaped like a T. But although it was realized that some support for the body under the feet or crutch must have been supplied, the *sedile* was not incorporated on the Cross of any Christian sect, perhaps for aesthetic reasons.

Although the *sedile* was not recorded in the Gospels, the

two positions on the cross are mirrored in the descriptions of the ordeal of Jesus. He spent some hours fully conscious and then, quite suddenly, collapsed and apparently died, remaining on the cross for another few hours before his body was taken down. The description of John, which includes the change from one position to the other, is:

> A jar stood there full of sour wine; so they soaked a sponge with the wine, fixed it on a javelin and held it up to his lips. Having received the wine, he said, 'It is accomplished!' He bowed his head and gave up his spirit [19: 29,30].

The last four words have an alternative translation, 'breathed out his life', added as a footnote in the New English Bible. The expression 'bowed his head' is interesting, but no alternative is given. The Greek verb used is *'klino'*; apart from 'to bow' it also means 'to lean', 'to cause to slant' or 'incline', words which would more exactly have described the way the head fell into the second position in the reconstructed experiment described in Chapter Six.

The Synoptics also say that Jesus remained dead on the cross for some time before being taken down. Mark and Matthew mention as well the offering of wine just before the change of position, and it is quite possible that the wine caused the sudden deterioration into unconsciousness. At this stage Jesus would have been extremely weak from his ordeal and could easily have choked on the liquid before lapsing into a coma.

The mystery as to why the man in the Shroud did not suffer the usual fate of the crucified, that of being left on the cross for animals to devour or thrown into a criminals' grave or lime-pit, is explained in the case of Jesus. All the Gospels report how Joseph of Arimathea, a respected member of the Sanhedrin, asked to be allowed to bury the body. He was reputedly wealthy – Matthew specifically states he was a man of means – and in John's Gospel he was accompanied by Nicodemus, who was said in the Talmud to be so rich he could have fed the entire population of Israel for eight days.[3] The expensive material of the Shroud ties in with the means of such men.

But there are other, more puzzling, features about the man in the cloth. For some reason his burial was not completed. He was placed naked in the cloth, unwashed and unanointed. Because it was such a disgrace to be left naked for ever, with his face covered, the circumstances surrounding the burial must have been most unusual.

This is precisely what they were in the case of Jesus. They are described most clearly in the Synoptics. The burial was only provisional, and it had to be accomplished quickly because of the impending Sabbath. All four Gospels mention this, but John states to the contrary that the full burial rites were carried out. The next chapter discusses why he differs from the others in this respect.

The Jewish Sabbath begins at sunset on Friday evening and ends with sunset on Saturday and in Jesus' time was observed with extraordinary strictness. The rules were laid down precisely, after interminable arguments among the rabbis, as to what constituted work and to what was therefore forbidden on the Lord's Day. For instance, it was a crime to crush a flea, but you might gently squeeze it or nip off a foot. An egg could not be eaten on the Sabbath day if the greater part of it had been laid by the hen before the second star was visible in the sky. Nor could false teeth be worn, or more than three amulets carried.[4] By the time the Mishna was compiled at the end of the second century, washing and anointing a dead body were allowed on the Sabbath, although none of the limbs was to be moved nor the eyes closed.[5] However, before the destruction of Jerusalem in AD 70 observance of the Sabbath was much stricter[6] and it would be no surprise if washing and anointing a body, as well as closing the eyes and moving a limb, would have constituted work.

It is impossible to be sure about the timing of the Crucifixion of Jesus, but working from the texts most scholars now believe that he was nailed to the cross at about midday, died at about three in the afternoon and was taken down from the cross for burial at about six. The blood-marks on the Shroud, with the two separate branches of the V on the wrist, would match this chronology very well. There was then only just time to carry out the simplest interment in the tomb before sunset.

There must have been a reason for the three hours between the apparent death of Jesus and his body being taken down. According to John it was some time after the death of Jesus that Joseph of Arimathea went to see Pilate. In Matthew and Mark Joseph did not go until the evening. In Mark, the earliest account, Pilate was so surprised to hear that Jesus had died so quickly that he sent for the centurion on Calvary to come and confirm it. Joseph then had to buy the linen sheet, and it must also be remembered that Pilate was a considerable distance from the site of Calvary, inside the city walls in the Antonia fortress or Herod's Palace. There was thus plenty to be done, including provision of burial materials: according to John, Nicodemus brought with him more than half a hundredweight of spices.

Another of the seemingly inexplicable conclusions drawn about the man in the cloth is therefore answered by the written accounts of Jesus. The possibility that they were one and the same person is thereby strengthened.

The man lay in the Shroud undisturbed long enough for the stains to form, in a trough-shaped space with soft material pillowing his head and pressing the cloth up against the soles of his feet. Exactly what shape Joseph's tomb was cannot be known for certain. It could certainly have produced the pattern of stains on the Shroud. Werner Bulst, in his book *The Shroud of Turin,* gave the dimensions of a typical tomb of a wealthy Jew of the Roman period, together with diagrams illustrating them, drawing on the researches of G. Dalmain, Director of the German Evangelical Institute in Jerusalem from 1902 to 1917. The receptacle for the corpse consisted of exactly the right sort of trough shape, with a wide rim all round. In this case, the height of the rim would have caused the cloth to fall back onto the body; but the back image of the Shroud suggests that the body was resting on sand, as mentioned in the Mishna, which would have raised it nearer the rim.

Also in the trough, according to the configuration of the stains on the cloth, were two piles of material: one under the head as a pillow, the other pressed between the feet and the end of the space.

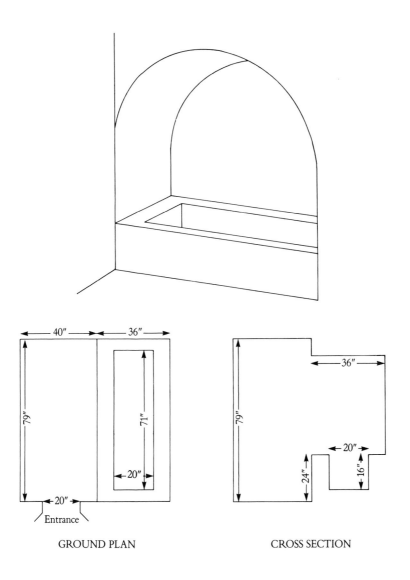

GROUND PLAN   CROSS SECTION

First-century tomb of a wealthy Jew. Based on Werner Bulst, *The Shroud of Turin* (1957).

Unfortunately, there are no written records describing how these two piles were placed in the tomb. However, in another of those graphic eye-witness sections in John, there is a description of how two piles of material were found there afterwards. Mary of Magdala, the first to find the empty tomb on the Sunday morning,

> ran to Simon Peter and the other disciple, the one whom Jesus loved. 'They have taken the Lord out of his tomb,' she cried, 'and we do not know where they have laid him.' So Peter and the other set out and made their way to the tomb. They were running side by side, but the other disciple outran Peter and reached the tomb first. He peered in and saw the linen wrappings lying there, but did not enter. Then Simon Peter came up, following him, and he went into the tomb. He saw the linen wrappings lying, and the napkin which had been over his head, not lying with the wrappings but rolled together in a place by itself. Then the disciple who had reached the tomb first went in too, and he saw and believed [20: 1-8].

There were clearly two separate piles of material in the tomb at this point, and they were bundled up rather than neatly folded. The impression given by the Greek is not that the body was spirited out of them leaving them undisturbed, but the opposite. Human interference is by no means ruled out.[7]

Presumably the piles of material were there all the time Jesus lay there, and this is another coincidence between the written accounts and the cloth. What the Gospels do not say is how they arrived there. It should be made clear that *neither* pile was the Shroud, for which the Greek word is *sindon*. This is the word used by the Synoptics in their descriptions of the burial. The word translated as 'napkin' in the passage quoted above, *sudarion*, implies a cloth for removing sweat, while that for the other pile, *othonia*, can be regarded as the generic plural for grave-clothes or grave-linen,[8] the materials used for the full burial rites.

Luke's Gospel is interesting. His Gospel, like Matthew's and Mark's, records that the body of Jesus was wrapped in a *sindon* (23,53). However he is the only one of the three to mention the contents of the empty tomb. In a verse which not all copyists included for some reason (24,12), after mentioning that the disciples did not believe the women's story when they returned from the tomb on the Sunday morning, he adds 'Peter, however, got up and ran to the tomb, and, peering in, saw the wrappings and nothing more.' Only *othonia*, with no sign of the *sindon*. Only grave wrappings; the Shroud had gone.

The written records do not state who placed these materials in the tomb, but we can perhaps speculate. Joseph of Arimathea, and Nicodemus if he was with him, may have taken the shroud to the tomb to carry out a provisional burial; they probably also took the spices necessary for the proper burial rites. If so, it is likely that they brought with them the other required materials – the linen *othonia* and *sudarion*. These would not have been left in the dust on the floor, where the heavy jar of spices probably stood. Instead, they could have been made into bundles, one being placed as a pillow for the shrouded head to lie on, the other between the feet and the end of the trough. In tucking the latter bundle under the feet they may have accidentally opened up the nail-wound, resulting in the jagged mark of fresh blood beside the heel. This is pure speculation, but it fits the facts and seems the most promising solution, for no one else is reported as having entered the tomb at the time of burial.

There was one other extraordinary conclusion drawn from the stains on the cloth. Although the man was in it long enough for the stains to develop, he was not there long enough for decay to begin. His body must have left the cloth when he was still alive or very soon after death. Here again the written evidence concerning Jesus matches perfectly, for he recovered and his recovery was witnessed by many people, who were able to touch his body and watch him eat and drink.

The coincidences are too great. The probability is that the body in the Shroud was Jesus's, fantastic though it seemed when first considered. Two quite independent witnesses corroborate each other: the Shroud vouches for the authenticity of the eye-witness in John at least as much as John identifies the man in the Shroud.

References

1.　Hengel, M., *Crucifixion,* S.C.M., 1977, p. 85.
2.　Priestland, G., *Yours Faithfully,* Collins, 1979, p. 133.
3.　Daniel-Rops, *Jesus in His Time,* Eyre and Spottiswoode, 1955, p. 161.
4.　Ibid, pp. 61, 212.
5.　O'Rahilly, A., *The Burial of Christ,* Cork University Press, 1942, p. 32.
6.　Leon-Dufour, X., *The Gospels and the Jesus of History,* Collins, 1968, p. 69.
7.　Robinson, J. A. T., *The Human Face of God,* S.C.M., 1973, p. 136.
8.　Robinson, J. A. T., 'The Shroud and the New Testament', in *Face to Face with the Turin Shroud,* ed. Peter Jennings, Matthew-McCrimmon and A. R. Mowbray, 1978, p. 70.

Ten

THE BODY LEAVES THE TOMB

'If there be no resurrection, then Christ was not raised; and if Christ was not raised, then our gospel is null and void, and so is your faith,' said Paul (1 Cor 15: 13). The fact that Jesus was dead on the Cross, and then appeared among the disciples alive again, is the cornerstone of the Christian faith.

It must have happened. The spread of the new religion proves it. Nothing but the certainty that they had witnessed the return of Jesus, who had overcome death, could have turned those early disciples – frightened, scattered, powerless men – into the creators of the Church of Christ. The question should not be *whether* it happened, but *how* it happened.

To many, the vast majority of Christians perhaps, the 'how' does not much matter. They simply accept the event in the same way as they accept the provision of light when they turn on the electric switch. Theirs is the sort of faith that is a gift. Others have to acquire it by reasoning, and therefore need to question.

For people with this urge, the standard explanation of the Resurrection poses a tremendous problem. They are told by the Church that the body of Jesus was the dead wreck of a human frame in the tomb one moment, and the next had been transformed into a live body again. It was substance – its wounds could be felt and it needed to eat and drink – but it

could pass through doors without opening them and
suddenly disappear again. Questioners puzzled by the way in
which these things happened receive a variety of unsatisfactory answers to their questions, most often: 'With God, all
things are possible.'

Except for those blessed with abiding faith, this will not
do. Experience and studies have shown that on this earth
there are certain laws that operate. Is the only answer really
that God stepped right outside those laws in the case of Jesus?

The study of the Shroud so far has shown that it could
have been formed naturally, even if the exact chemical
reaction is not yet known. The stage has been reached where
Jesus's body was in the tomb, in a deep coma, on the Friday
night. By Sunday morning, the tomb was empty. Only the
two piles of linen remained. The body *and the Shroud* had
disappeared.

Immediately one snag with the supernatural theory is
apparent. If the body of Jesus was transformed, what
happened to the Shroud?

That problem has already been considered at length by
scholars. It has been suggested that either the word *sudarion*
or *othonia* could, under certain circumstances, mean a shroud.
This explanation ignores a practical point. The Shroud
would have been left along the full length of the ledge had the
body supernaturally dematerialized. The *sudarion* and the
othonia were bundled up. If one of those was the Shroud,
who bundled it up? Further the stains show that when the
Shroud was round the body both piles of material were
already in place.

That Jesus may have been in a coma in the tomb and
recovered naturally is a very old suggestion, but as far I know
it has always been mooted that he would have left the tomb
unaided. The forensic scientists and doctors I have consulted
do not consider this physically possible. In any case, D. F.
Strauss in the last century pointed out the flaw in this
argument:

> It is impossible that a being who had stolen half-dead out of the
> sepulchre, weak and ill, wanting treatment and bandaging, could
> have given the disciples the impression that he was the

conqueror of death and the grave, the Prince of Life; an impression that lay at the bottom of their future ministry.

That leaves one alternative: the body and the Shroud were removed from the grave by somebody. The question arises as to who it could have been.

Someone unconnected with Jesus is really out of the question. Body-snatchers would have had no motive in the years before artists and surgeons paid handsomely for bodies; and although grave-robbers might have taken the rich material, they would have been far more interested in the jar of spices than the body. Neither the Jewish nor the Roman authorities would have moved it to another tomb, for when the disciples began to claim that Jesus had risen from the dead the body would have been produced immediately.

This leaves Jesus's friends, in particular the disciples. The latter might have wished to render a final service to their Master by transferring his body from the grave of the Councillor, Joseph of Arimathea, to one they had prepared themselves and proposed to venerate. When they removed the body and Shroud on the Saturday night, they would have found it in a strange state, and after being nursed for a while it could have revived. But the argument of Strauss quoted above would still apply. The Gospels also report that most of the disciples were scattered, and the account of the finding of the tomb on the Sunday morning by St Peter and St John would make no sense if we accept this explanation. Finally, Christianity would have been established on a guilty secret, which is inconceivable. Whoever took the body must have been a friend of Jesus, but was not in communication with the disciples. This brings us once again to Joseph of Arimathea.

Several writers have suggested that Jesus's body was removed by Joseph, partly because there is a description in the apocryphal Acts of Pilate or the Gospel of Nicodemus, of his trial before the Council on this very charge. There was an obvious motive for his action: the nearness of sunset compelled him to bury Jesus in his own private tomb nearby, but as soon as the Sabbath was over he perhaps intended moving it elsewhere. This is possible, but unlikely. He must have had a quite remarkable reverence for Jesus to have begged his body from Pilate for burial, and would not have refused him the permanent use of his own tomb.

One point must be emphasized: begging the body of Jesus from Pilate and burying it were acts of very great courage and would certainly have drawn the anger of his fellow-councillors, for apart from removing the responsibility for the disposal of the body from the Romans, Joseph left the body where it was vulnerable to theft by the disciples. Not only that, his actions would have been inexplicable to his peers. Jesus was a Galilean, had been a manual labourer, had falsely claimed to be the Messiah and, since crucifixion, was accursed of God. For a fellow-councillor to stoop to burying such a man would have seemed inconceivable.

The social divisions of the time were extremely wide. More than nine-tenths of the Palestinian Jews were labelled as the people of the land, the *am ha-arez*. The orthodox could not eat or associate with them, and the severity of this attitude can be judged from this quotation from the Talmud:

> No man may marry the daughter of the *am ha-arez*, for they are like unclean animals, and their wives like reptiles, and it is concerning their daughters that Scripture says: 'Cursed be he who lies with any kind of beast' [Deuteronomy 27: 21].[2]

Such was the hatred of such people that the rabbis unanimously agreed that even on the Sabbath it was permissible to use a knife on the *am ha-arez*.[3] The feelings concerning Galileans would have compounded the dislike, for the qualification 'Galilean' was synonymous with a cursed, lawless rabble.[4]

It was among these outcasts that Jesus had worked, regarding them as sheep without a shepherd, and it was this, as well as his failure to observe scrupulously some of the Pharisaic rules, such as washing hands before eating, that ensured he was regarded with animosity by the religious leaders.[5]

It would have taken considerable courage to question this disdain in the Sanhedrin, but Nicodemus did so. There is a section in John's Gospel that brings out these points clearly.

The chief priests and Pharisees had sent the Temple police to arrest Jesus.

> The temple police came back to the chief priests and Pharisees, who asked, 'Why have you not brought him?' 'No man', they answered, 'ever spoke as this man speaks.' The Pharisees retorted, 'Have you too been misled? Is there a single one of our rulers who has believed in him, or of the Pharisees? As for this rabble, which cares nothing for the Law, a curse is on them.' Then one of their number, Nicodemus (the man who had once visited Jesus), intervened. 'Does our law', he asked them, 'permit us to pass judgement on a man unless we have first given him a hearing and learned the facts?' 'Are you a Galilean too?' they retorted. 'Study the scriptures and you will find that prophets do not come from Galilee.' [7: 45-52]

The background detail emphasizes how extraordinary – and dangerous – it was for Joseph and Nicodemus to bury the body of Jesus. In the first place, as previously mentioned, it needed a great deal of courage to beg for the body from Pilate, an unpredictable tyrant according to the historians. But they were also putting their friends and much more at risk by performing this service to a man who was, to the Council, an accursed Galilean impostor.

If they were willing to risk so much to bury the man they revered, it is most unlikely that they would have done it inadequately. They must have been intending to give the body the full rites, and it would have been unthinkable to have abandoned it for ever in a state of ritual impurity.

It is recorded that on the Friday evening they put the body in the Shroud provisionally, but they probably also brought the required grave-linen together with a large quantity of spices. They *must* have intended to finish off the process as soon as the Sabbath was over. The women had to wait until light on the Sunday morning, but Joseph and Nicodemus could have come any time after sunset on the Saturday.

When they reached the tomb and stripped off the top of the cloth, it would have been clear that the body was unlike normal corpses. To begin with, its skin would have been at a higher temperature than the surroundings. There would have been diaphragmatic breathing which might just have been visible on the lips or nose. The body might also have coughed, or jerked a limb. If so, they would not have left it unguarded in the tomb. Nothing is more likely than their deciding to take it away, covered with the Shroud for warmth, to tend it and await developments. The grave-linen would not be needed, so they left it on the ledge in its two piles.

That is how the mistake could have arisen. The women had watched the provisional burial. They would not have dared speak to the councillors: they were women, as well as Galileans and *am ha-arez*. They could not be sure Joseph and Nicodemus would lower themselves even further and return to finish off the burial rites, so they prepared to do it themselves. When Mary found the grave empty on the Sunday morning, she reported to the disciples, 'They have taken the Lord out of his tomb, and we do not know where they have laid him.'

St John had not witnessed the interment. At about three o'clock Jesus had committed his mother to St John's care, and as soon as Jesus had died he would have hurried her from that distressing sight. He was not to know how those three hours had been taken up. He assumed the body had been prepared properly by Joseph and Nicodemus. 'They took the body of Jesus', says his Gospel (19: 40), 'and wrapped it, with the spices, in strips of linen cloth according to Jewish burial-customs.' And when he saw those two piles on the Sunday morning, he assumed that they had come off the body, 'and he saw and believed; until then they had not understood the scriptures, which showed that he must rise again from the dead' (John 20: 9).

The supernatural explanation was born. But the natural one is just as remarkable.

References

1. Morison, F., *Who Moved the Stone?* Faber and Faber, (1944 ed.), p. 92.
2. Vermes, G., *Jesus the Jew,* Fontana/Collins, 1976, pp. 54, 55.
3. Daniel-Rops, *Jesus in His Time,* Eyre and Spottiswoode, 1955, p. 134.

4. Vermes, G., op. cit., p. 33.
5. Metzger, B., *The New Testament, its Background, Growth and Content,* Lutterworth Press, 1969, p. 46.

Eleven
PERIPHERAL PROBLEMS

There are still problems, when the Gospel accounts are studied, but none are insuperable and reasonable explanations can be found for all of them.

One question that occurs to anyone familiar with Matthew's Gospel concerns the guard. Soldiers were detailed to the tomb on the Saturday morning to prevent anyone taking the body away. How, then, could Joseph and Nicodemus have removed it?

It is quite possible, in fact, that there was *no* guard. Our only source on this point is Matthew, whose motives may have been either to counter rumours that the body had been removed by the disciples, or to emphasize the miraculous element. The latter suggestion is supported by his account of what happened when the women came to the tomb on the Sunday morning:

> The Sabbath had passed, and it was about daybreak on Sunday, when Mary of Magdala and the other Mary came to look at the grave. Suddenly there was a violent earthquake; an angel of the Lord descended from heaven; he came to the stone and rolled it away, and sat himself down on it. His face shone like lightning; his garments were white as snow. At the sight of him the guards shook with fear and lay like the dead. The angel then addressed the women . . . [Matthew 28: 1-5].

There are touches here of a vivid imagination that was concerned to stress the supernatural possibilities of the scene. Compare it with Mark's description, on which it was probably based:

> When the Sabbath was over, Mary of Magdala, Mary the mother of James, and Salome brought aromatic oils intending to go and anoint him; and very early on the Sunday morning, just after sunrise, they came to the tomb. They were wondering among themselves who would roll away the stone for them from the entrance to the tomb, when they looked up and saw that the stone, huge as it was, had been rolled back already. They went into the tomb, where they saw a youth sitting on the right-hand side, wearing a white robe; and they were dumbfounded. But he said to them . . . [Mark 16: 1-6].

So the guard could well have been an invention of Matthew. When the tomb in which Jesus's body had been placed was discovered to be empty, rumours would have begun that the disciples had stolen it. Joseph of Arimathea was accused of that before the Sanhedrin, according to the Acts of Pilate, but such a mundane explanation of the body's disappearance would not have been acceptable to many of Jesus's followers, and therefore Matthew may well have invented the soldiers to counter the suggestion.

On the other hand it is possible that a guard was placed to prevent the theft of the body and that this was known only to the source of Matthew's Gospel. In this case, judging from the other Gospels, they must have left before the women arrived at the tomb. What caused them to leave?

There are several possible explanations. The most plausible involve their entering the tomb for some reason. This may have been simply a routine check or because they heard a noise made by the comatose body; or, most likely, for theft. The quantity of spices in the tomb was an extremely valuable commodity, which they would have noted when sealing the tomb on the Saturday morning. The temptation to steal some may have occurred to them then and increased during the long day, so that they agreed to go in and remove some under cover of darkness. It would have been an unnerving venture with any corpse there; but with Jesus's reputation as a miracle-worker, so much the worse. If the body had jerked or coughed, or if they had simply seen a slight movement of the cloth from the minimal breathing, they would certainly have fled. However, it is more likely that there was no guard. It was Joseph and Nicodemus who rolled back the stone when they came to the tomb, and they left it open to be found by the women.

There is very little the Shroud can suggest about what happened afterweards. The man could have revived at any time, or died. As no bones were broken, a long convalescence would not have been required. Nevertheless, careful tending would have been necessary, and it might have taken perhaps three weeks for him to have reached a good, walking fitness. This may be a considerable over-estimate based on modern doctors' experience of pampered, overfed Europeans. A doctor who served in the Yemen for a number of years suggested that we under-estimate the strength and capacity for pain of people in that area. Living a hardy life, eating millet predominantly, their bodies are much lighter than Western men with similar physiques, and they can stand severe injuries without showing great pain. People would come to his surgery with wounds that would have killed their European counterparts, or at any rate left them prostrate for months. Their powers of recovery were equally impressive, and no doubt the same was true of their ancestors.

The Shroud, however, cannot provide clues about what happened next, which has to be speculation based on the written records.

Unfortunately, these sections of the Gospels are not only surprisingly scanty, considering the crucial importance of the Resurrection to the early Church, but contradictory. In Matthew all the appearances of Jesus were in Galilee; in Luke they were all in Jerusalem. In John they were in both, while Mark mentions none at all. An attempt has been made to harmonize the appearances, making Jesus appear in Jerusalem on Easter Day (Luke, John) and also eight days later (John), then in Galilee (Matthew, John) and finally in Jerusalem at the moment of the Ascension (Luke); but the individual written records have to be twisted considerably to fit in with this.[1] There are contradictions even between the two accounts by the same author, for Luke, in Acts 1:3, has Jesus appearing to his disciples 'over a period of forty days', whereas in Luke 24 the Ascension apparently took place on Easter Day.

The reason for these significant discrepancies is not known. Since Mark's Gospel finishes at 16:8 – the verses that follow were later additions by a different author – Matthew and Luke were unable to draw on him. They had to find their own sources, and these did not match.

As historical evidence for the Resurrection, the written records are not strong. Yet it is clear from the accounts that it was not the evidence of the empty tomb that was felt to be. important, but the actual physical presence of Jesus. To sense this, one has only to read the description of the early Church in Acts. The section in John, where doubting Thomas is encouraged to feel Jesus's wounds, is equally convincing, and in Luke also Jesus is remembered as being too solid for a spirit.

> Startled and terrified, they thought they were seeing a ghost. But he said, 'Why are you so perturbed? Why do questionings arise in your minds? Look at my hands and feet. It is I myself. Touch me and see; no ghost has flesh and bones as you can see that I have'. They were still unconvinced, still wondering, for it seemed too good to be true. So he asked them, 'Have you had anything to eat?' They offered him a piece of fish they had cooked, which he took and ate before their eyes [Luke 24: 37-43].

Jesus's solidity is also obvious in the following excerpt from Paul's first letter to the Corinthians:

> First and foremost, I handed on to you the facts that were imparted to me: that Christ died for our sins, in accordance with the scriptures; that he was buried; that he was raised to life on the third day, according to the scriptures; and that he appeared to Cephas, and afterwards to the Twelve. Then he appeared to over five hundred of our brothers at once, most of whom are still alive, though some have died. Then he appeared to James, and

afterwards to all the apostles [1 Cor. 15: 3-7].

Deducing from such imprecise clues is difficult, but there are two fixed points from which a start can be made. In the course of years memories can become increasingly distorted, as mentioned earlier, unless tied to fixed points such as festivals. It is fortunate in this respect that the Crucifixion took place at Passover and the triumphant announcement in Jerusalem that Jesus had risen from being dead at Pentecost, seven weeks later. There is another reason why these dates are practically certain, for from the very beginning Passover and Pentecost were the only two Jewish feasts observed as holy days by the early Christian Church.[2]

This seven-week gap has mystified scholars, for if the timetable suggested in various Gospel acounts is correct, all Jerusalem would have known about the Resurrection within a day or two. Luke cannot be right about those appearances in Jerusalem, or the suggestion that Jesus was seen by the disciples on the way to Emmaus on Easter Sunday.

If the deductions from the Shroud are correct, Jesus was recovering, in the care of Joseph or Nicodemus, for some time after his body left the tomb on the Saturday night. If any of his disciples did linger near Jerusalem after the Crucifixion, they would have left for Galilee after a few days, disappointed and distraught, convinced that their Master had been extinguished by death.

The seven-week gap makes sense then. What possibly happened was this. Jesus must have recovered consciousness soon after removal from the tomb. He specifically prophesied that he would be three days in his ordeal – in three days he was to rebuild the temple of his body, and by the sign of Jonah, the Son of Man was to be three days and three nights in the bowels of the earth (Matthew 12: 40) – and that prophecy would have been precisely fulfilled if he came round on the Monday evening. His victory over death is celebrated on Easter Sunday simply because the tomb was discovered empty that morning, but perhaps his victory came later. Whenever he recovered, he would have needed perhaps as long as three weeks to build up his strength. He then set out for Galilee.

This is when he may have passed through Emmaus. It is no surprise that Cleopas and the other disciple failed to recognize him at first: not only were they sure he was dead, but extreme suffering can radically alter appearances. Further north he may well have visited his home, for James his brother, who was not previously a disciple, became a prominent one after this time. And so to the Sea of Galilee, the shepherd rounding up his scattered sheep. Perhaps several of the disciples were fishing and saw Jesus on the shore, as in that final fragment of the 'disciple whom Jesus loved' in John 21. There is no way of knowing. The one certainty is that he did join them, and they were convinced he had conquered death and was with them again in the flesh. And in this short time with them, he fired them with the power, the enthusiasm, and the conviction to establish the Church that was to spread throughout the world.

He left his disciples then. It was now up to them, and Jerusalem was where they began their ministry. So it was that after seven weeks they entered the city they had left so dejectedly and fired the Pentecost crowds with the ecstatic announcement that Jesus had risen from the dead and was the Messiah.

The recorded appearances that do not agree with this chronology may be explained by the period it took Jesus to recover and the decades that elapsed before the Gospels were written.

The unreliability of the records as regards the precise timing of these events has already been mentioned. The Evangelists were not historians, and the exact reporting of dates and times did not matter to them. The effect of the passing years on memories also has to be borne in mind. But there is a third factor: the number of people who passed on an account before it was finally set down in writing. The story of Jesus joining Cleopas and the other disciple on the way to Emmaus provides a good example. Luke states specifically that it occurred on 'that same day', the Sunday that is. But the Gospel was not written down for thirty or forty years after the event. The story probably passed through many mouths on the way.

Yet it reads so impressively that it must surely have

happened; indeed, it was probably the first appearance of Jesus to any of the disciples. Because of this, it was probably described early on as occurring 'not long after he came to life again'. After a few years this could easily have become 'soon after'; and for this to change to 'that same day' after another decade or two is not at all surprising.

The passage of time and the passing of the message from one person to another would have caused the accounts to alter; but it was the changing view of the nature of Jesus that resulted in such alterations being given supernatural colouring. The thirst of Jesus's pious followers for wonderful details of his life and death led to the production of the Apocryphal Gospels as the years passed, and bizarre, miraculous details were written down and believed. By the middle of the second century the story of the guard in Matthew's Gospel, quoted at the beginning of this chapter, had been elaborated to the following pitch in the *Gospel of Peter*:

> Now in the night whereon the Lord's day dawned, as the soldiers were keeping guard two by two in every watch, there came a great sound in the heaven, and they saw the heavens opened and two men descend thence, shining with a great light, and drawing near unto the sepulchre. And that stone which had been set on the door rolled away of itself and went back to the side, and the sepulchre was opened and both of the young men entered in. When therefore the soldiers saw that, they waked up the centurion and the elders (for they also were there keeping watch): and while they were yet telling them the things which they had seen, they saw again three men come out of the sepulchre, and two of them sustaining the other, and a cross following after them. And of the two they saw that their heads reached unto heaven, but of him that was led by them that it overpassed the heavens. And they heard a voice out of the heavens saying: Hast thou preached unto them that sleep? And an answer was heard from the cross, saying: Yea.[3]

Although this and similar works were not included in the canonical New Testament, they enjoyed considerable popularity in the Middle Ages.[4] Apart from their errors of taste, they show just how much embellishment and exaggeration can be added by the pious faithful.

That same tendency must be present in the Gospel accounts, though to a lesser extent. It is in the post-Resurrection appearances that we are perhaps most likely to encounter elaborations. One of the disciples perhaps remembered how they were all seated in a room when, to their great surprise, Jesus suddenly came in through the door. A natural enough description, but the first hearer could so easily have misunderstood the exact message, or added an embellishing touch to imply that Jesus had passed through the door without opening it.

The stories that have Jesus appearing to the women at the tomb do not of course fit with the theory that he recovered elsewhere after his body had been removed. These stories may well have begun with rumours. Consider the situation in Jerusalem on the Sunday. Jesus, the remarkable Galilean rabbi who was also a great healer and seemed especially favoured by God, had been crucified two days before, but a report was circulating that in some mysterious way his body had disappeared from its tomb. This was exciting news, and in such an atmosphere rumours would have been quickly generated and eagerly received. His disciples had found the grave-clothes in the tomb, it was said, and were saying that he must have risen from the dead! Where was he then? No one was sure. Apparently, his women followers had been the first to the tomb, so *they* may have seen him. Mary of Magdala was their leader and had been a favourite of his. Perhaps *she* had seen him. But the grave-linen was reportedly left in the tomb. What then, did he wear? Ah, but it was a garden tomb, and the gardener had left some clothes there that he had been able to put on, which explained why Mary had not recognized him at first.

Such rumours could have formed easily amidst the excitement. When there was no sign of Jesus himself, and excitement lessened and was slowly transformed into deep disappointment, they would have been forgotten. But then, at Pentecost, the firm news broke: Jesus had indeed risen from the dead! He had gone immediately northwards to Galilee to be with his disciples, and here they were, spreading the news with complete conviction. The rumours were then revived, and as the belief grew that Jesus had risen mysteriously, supernaturally, these rumours became arguments for authenticity and placed on an equal footing with the genuine reports.

In view of the change in the way Jesus was regarded during the intervening years, it is surprising that the stories in the Gospel accounts are not even more spectacular.

References

1. Leon-Dufour, X., *The Gospels and the Jesus of History*, Collins, 1968, pp. 255-257.
2. Ibid., p. 260.
3. James, M. R., *The Apocryphal New Testament*, Oxford University Press, 1953, p. 92.
4. Daniel-Rops, *Jesus in his Time*, Eyre and Spottiswoode, 1956, pp. 25-28.

Twelve

SEARCHING BEHIND THE IMAGES

It is fortunate that St Peter's first sermon, given on the Day of Pentecost, is preserved in the Acts of the Apostles. Here we can see how Jesus was regarded soon after his return to life. 'Men of Israel, listen to me,' Peter cried.

> I speak of Jesus of Nazareth, a man singled out by God and made known to you through miracles, portents, and signs, which God worked among you through him, as you well know. When he had been given up to you, by the deliberate will and plan of God, you used heathen men to crucify and kill him. But God raised him to life again, setting him free from the pangs of death, because it could not be that death should keep him in its grip. [Acts 2:22-24]

A man singled out by God. All the Jews in Jerusalem must have regarded Jesus in this way. He had lived among them and they had known and observed him as a man. A man singled out by God, as was shown by the miracles, portents and signs, culminating in his recovery from death. But still a man.

Yet, in the years to come, he was to lose that description. He was to become a part of God, the second Person of the Trinity, co-existent with the other two eternal Persons of

God – the Father and the Holy Ghost. His role, too, became more complicated. Although still a part of God, he became a man, having both natures at once. He did this so that he could suffer death at the hands of men, in order that God the Father could forgive man his other sins.

The development of this change of view is apparent in the four Gospels. The order in which they were written was almost certainly Mark, Matthew, Luke, and finally John. Although Mark was not written for at least twenty years after the Crucifixion, Jesus was still regarded mainly as a rounded human being. But by the time Matthew and Luke were writing, and using Mark as a source, reverence for Jesus had increased. This comes out in the texts. For example, Mark only once uses 'the Lord' in reference to him (Mark 11: 3), but Luke uses it sixteen times and Matthew nineteen. Human emotions in Mark's account – such as grief and anger (Mark 3: 5), amazement (Mark 6: 6) and unrequited love (Mark 10: 21) – are suppressed or weakened by the other two, and they omit the suggestion that Jesus's friends thought he was beside himself (Mark 3: 21). These may seem petty alterations, but they are clear signs of a change in attitude, and there are others. For instance, Matthew and Luke allow none of the human weaknesses mentioned by Mark, such as ignorance of certain points, or an inability to enter a certain town. And they add touches of the miraculous not in Mark's original stories. For example, whereas in Mark (1: 32-34) 'they brought to him *all* who were ill or possessed by devils . . . He healed *many* who suffered from various diseases, and drove out *many* devils' (my emphasis), in Matthew (8: 16-17) this becomes: 'they brought to him many who were possessed by devils: and he drove the spirits out *with a word* and healed *all* who were ill . . .'.[1] Similarly, Mark 6: 5-6; 'He could work no miracle there, except that he put his hands on a few sick people and healed them; and he was taken aback by their want of faith', becomes in Matthew 13:58: 'And he did not work many miracles there: such was their want of faith.' The suggestion that Jesus could not do something is subtly avoided, as is the possibility that he could be surprised. There are plenty of similar examples.[2]

The change from Mark to Matthew and Luke was

considerable, but the gap between them and the Fourth Gospel is immense. Jesus is no longer a man at all. He claims he is God, and existed before Abraham. He is the Resurrection and the Life; the Way, the Truth and the Life, and the Son of Man who came down from Heaven.[3] These and many other claims dissolve the humanity from him. He has been elevated right out of reach.

The passage of time is not a sufficient explanation. There must be some other factor. To see what this might be, the situation as Christianity began to spread must be considered.

The early Church was strictly controlled from Jerusalem, where Peter, James and John were the main authorities. Surprisingly, James, the brother of Jesus, was pre-eminent. The authorised version of Jesus, so to speak, was therefore disseminated from Jerusalem and this predominantly Jewish Church, firmly monotheistic, would have rejected any suggestion that he was a god. He was acknowledged as having fulfilled the role of Messiah, but although many different types of Messiah had been anticipated by Jews in the past, none had been divine in the sense of being a second God. He was expected to be a man, though a singular and heroic figure.[4] The division between him and God is shown by the ancient liturgies, which talk about 'Jesus, thy servant' and 'through Jesus, thy beloved servant.'[5]

In the meantime, Paul was teaching a revised version to the Gentiles that was fundamentally different. It did not have the authority of the apostles in Jerusalem, nor did Paul feel it was needed, for his inspiration came directly from God. To the Galatians he writes:

> I must make it clear to you, my friends, that the gospel you heard me preach is no human invention. I did not take it over from any man; I received it through a revelation of Jesus Christ.
> You have heard what my manner of life was when I was still a practising Jew: how savagely I persecuted the church of God, and tried to destroy it . . . But then in his good pleasure God, who had set me apart from birth and called me through his grace, chose to reveal his Son to me and through me, in order that I might proclaim him among the Gentiles. When that happened, without consulting any human being, without going up to Jerusalem to see those who were apostles before me, I went off at once . . . [Galatians 1: 12-17].

Paul's concrete faith in the value of his calling stands out in this epistle and elsewhere. He describes himself in the heading of this letter as 'an apostle, not by human appointment or human commission, but by commission from Jesus Christ and from God the Father who raised him from the dead', and the same firm conviction in his calling shines through all his letters. But so does his sense that, because of this calling, he alone was qualified to preach the Gospel to the Gentiles. Others did not have his commission from God. He wrote his letter to the Galatians because they were inclining towards the authorised version from Jerusalem. Not allowed! 'If anyone . . . should preach a gospel at variance with the one we preached to you, he shall be held outcast.'

Paul has scant respect for the apostles in Jerusalem. He calls them 'those reputed pillars of our society, James, Cephas, and John'. And while he was happy for them to preach their gospel to the Jews, he was not going to have his Gentiles affected by it.

Nevertheless, he recognized their authority as the centre of the universal Church, and raised money abroad to send back to it. Also, as he told the Galatians, he felt that he had to go to Jerusalem to explain what he was preaching.

> But as for the men of high reputation (not that their importance matters to me: God does not recognize these personal distinctions) – these men of repute, I say, did not prolong the consultation, but on the contrary acknowledged that I had been entrusted with the Gospel for Gentiles as surely as Peter had been entrusted with the Gospel for Jews. For God whose action made Peter an apostle to the Jews, also made me an apostle to the Gentiles [Galatians 2: 6-8].

There were thus two Gospels, and whereas in Jerusalem they were remembering the man they had seen and known and who had come as the Messiah, Paul – who had never seen Jesus – defended his authority on the basis of divine revelation. He discouraged interest in the historical Jesus in favour of mystical communion with the Risen.Christ.[6] 'With us,' he tells the men of Corinth, 'worldly standards have ceased to count in our estimate of any man; even if once they counted in our estimate of Christ, they do so no longer. When anyone is united to Christ, there is a new world, the old order has gone, and the new order has already begun.' Interest in Christ as a man was irrelevant, the crucifixion was a mystical event, and the victim was a divine being, 'the Lord of Glory'.

Such were the differences between the two Gospels.

Acts 21 and 22 describe what happened when eventually Paul came up to Jerusalem to meet the leaders of the Church there. The whole city was in uproar, and Paul only escaped death by being rescued by the Romans and smuggled out of the city. Already there was a deep division between the first two branches of Christianity.

But soon only one survived. In the four disastrous years of the Jewish Revolt, the Jerusalem Church was destroyed. Its supreme authority over the Jewish and Gentile Christian communities loosened and then was completely severed. The group of original witnesses and disciples was decimated and then scattered. The memories they had of Jesus, and there may have been a considerable quantity of written records, were lost to the world. Paul's Gentiles assumed control, and although the arguments and doctrinal struggles continued bitterly, it was his theology that provided the dogma. It was therefore the destruction of the Jerusalem Church that was the key to the change in the view of Christ in Christianity as a whole.

For those brought up with these developed beliefs of Christ's nature, stripping off the layers to get to the core is extremely difficult. Going back from Paul and John, through Luke and Matthew to Mark, is the simplest part. But Mark's Gospel was probably written about thirty years after the death of Jesus, so that to get back to his real nature requires even more extrapolation, which can lead to errors. The line descends from Paul's God on earth to Peter's man singled out by God; but precisely what sort of man cannot be established with certainty.

For reasons already mentioned, the best primary source is probably the teaching of Jesus, for this would have been handed on by the oral tradition fairly accurately over many years. Here John's Gospel is the least valuable, Mark's the most reliable.

In some places in the Gospels, when Jesus describes himself, directly or indirectly, one phrase is repeated by which he clearly wishes to be remembered: the son of man. It occurs eighty-one times in the Gospels, and in eighty of those passages the phrase is used by Jesus himself. In the one exception, John 12: 34, the people are echoing his words. This is highly significant. By the time the Gospels were written, the phrase did not fit the belief that Jesus was divine, and the Gospel writers also knew that the title was not clear to the Gentiles. The one reason they recorded it was because Jesus actually used those words.[7] As for the meaning of the phrase, in Jewish Aramaic it often meant simply 'man'.[8] Although it is found in a different sense in Daniel 7:13, there is no evidence that Jesus used it in a similar way.[9]

If Jesus emphasizes his humanity with that expression, he also makes clear that God is on a different plane. His great prayer is directed to 'Our Father in Heaven' (Matthew 6: 9), and this distinction is similarly emphasized when he answers the lawyer's question: 'Which commandment is first of all?'

> 'The first is, "Hear O Israel: the Lord your God is the only Lord; love the Lord your God with all your heart, with all your soul, with all your mind, and with all your strength." The second is this: "Love your neighbour as yourself." There is no other commandment greater than these.' [Mark 12: 29-31]

Another clear indication in the words of Jesus that he did not think of himself as God appears in his answer to the rich man in Mark's Gospel (10:18). 'Why do you call me good? No one is good but God alone.' Only as a man could he have said this.

But perhaps the distinction is most starkly seen in the final cry on the Cross: 'My God, my God, why hast though forsaken me?' There can be no doubt that he cried out those words. Why else would they be remembered? They were the greatest possible contradiction to the growing belief in his divinity. Nor were they muttered, as if he was reciting the first words of Psalm 22. He cried them aloud, so memorably that they are given in the Aramaic syllables that cut deep into the memories of those who heard them.

Not only was Jesus a man, but he was a Jew. He thought and expressed himself as a Jew, and such was his faith in the Jewish beliefs and scriptures that he was willing to offer his life as a religious sacrifice. He felt that he was called to redeem his nation and intended his death to atone for its sins in the same way as the scapegoat driven from Jerusalem each year. As a Jew he felt himself to be a member of the Chosen Race, and his mission was to them rather than Gentiles.[10] This attitude shows clearly in his recorded words, which compare Gentiles with pigs and dogs in places,[11] and his instructions to his disciples to give preference to the Jews.[12] These reports must be authentic, since the universal Church would doubtless have found them an embarrassment. Long after his death, the Jerusalem Church even doubted whether his message was intended for the Gentiles: this must have been the result of the influence of Jesus during his life.[13]

Not only was he a pure Jew, but he was a first-century Jew. His medical ideas were those existing then, so that schizophrenia, epilepsy and other ailments were devils to be exorcized. The pictures painted in some of his parables, too, were strictly of his time, and this applies most obviously to his concept of physical resurrection, with men entering heaven without the offending eye or the foot previously amputated.

Thus a man, a first-century Jew, is revealed as the basis of the portrait, but there were special aspects to him as well. There is no doubt that as a healer and exorcist he was remarkable, though others were probably equally so. Where he is unique is in the brilliance of his words. Right through his recorded teaching, his parables, sermons and conversation, shines the inspiration that came to him from the God he worshipped and interpreted. It infected the crowds around him, and through him they glimpsed eternal truths.

The written records of the New Testament do provide a portrait of Jesus, but only the much retouched outer layer is obvious. It is not possible to strip off those layers to discover the original portrait; but a certain amount can be revealed, resembling the way X-rays and other techniques can examine the basis of an old master painting. Underneath is the man, singled out by God, and he has been described by Professor Hick in a way that could hardly be bettered:[14]

> He was a man who was intensely conscious of God, living continuously in God's presence and finding his meat and drink in the doing of God's work on earth. His life was so transparent to the divine will that he could speak about the heavenly Father with authority, could proclaim His forgiveness, and could declare His claim upon men; and the power of life flowed through his hands in healing. He was so vividly aware of God that in his presence men and women were drawn by spiritual contagion into the conscious presence of God. In this way he was a saviour to many, and continues to be so today through the living memory of him passed down to us in the New Testament and within the Christian community.

References

1. Metzger, B., *The New Testament, its Background, Growth and Content*, Lutterworth Press, 1969, p. 80.
2. Mitton, C. L., *Jesus: the Fact behind the Faith*, Mowbray, 1975, pp. 42-46.
3. Hanson, R. P. C., 'The unexamined assumption of most Christian believers', *The Times*, 10 June 1978.
4. Brandon, S. G. F., *The Fall of Jerusalem and the Christian Church*, S.P.C.K., 1951, p. 79.
5. Cullmann, O., *The Christology of the New Testament*, S.C.M., 1963, p. 75.
6. Brandon, S. G. F., *The Trial of Jesus of Nazareth*, Batsford, 1968, pp. 18, 19.
7. Filson, F. V., *A New Testament History*, S.C.M. 1965, p. 78.
8. Dodd, C. H., *The Founder of Christianity*, Collins, 1971, p. 111.
9. Vermes, G., *Jesus the Jew*, Fontana/Collins, 1976, p. 185.
10. Dodd, C. H., op. cit., Chapter 5
11. Matthew 7:6; Mark 7:27; Matthew 15:26.
12. Matthew 10: 5-6; Matthew 15:24.
13. Vermes, G., op. cit., p. 49. Acts 10.
14. Hick, J., 'Changing views of the uniqueness of Christ', *The Times*, 11 October 1975.

Thirteen
ROLES

As we have seen in the last chapter, although the earliest Gospel was written twenty or thirty years after the Crucifixion of Jesus, there are still enough clues to see the man behind the varnish. His words show that he was very much a Jew of the first century, conscious of his mission to his own, the Chosen Race. His deeds too betray his humanity; touches of temper such as the cursing of the fig tree, as well as the indication that he was not able to cure all who came to him.[1] To suggest, as additional evidence, that he justified his reputation as a sinner is perhaps putting it too strongly; but the Gospels report how he was thought to be a glutton and a drinker and yet, surprisingly, do not deny it.[2] There is a genuine human touch there perhaps.

If his complete humanity is accepted, it is the depth of his knowledge of God that matters as much as anything. How did it come to him? Did he see God? Hear His voice?

Studying the Synoptic Gospels with this in mind, one gets the impression that Jesus had no methods of communication with God beyond those open to any man. He had to rely on prayer, and the inspired words of the Scriptures. He was a channel for God's words, in the line of the Prophets, but this does not mean he had a 'hot line' to God that allowed the accuracy of two-way conversation. He had the same difficulties, the same doubts, the same possibilities of error that all men have.

Certainly he tried to interpret God's will, but he did not give his disciples confidence in his predictions. He was known as a prophet to the people, but this was more in the sense of wonder-worker than a foreteller of the future,[3] and hardly any instances of his historical predictions are recorded. One, concerning the destruction of Jerusalem in AD 70, is suspect as the Gospels were probably written down after the event occurred. Others are obscure. However, one is quite specific: that the *Parousia*, by which was meant his second coming and the establishment of the Kingdom of Heaven, would occur soon after his death. Read Mark Chapter 13 to sense the whole vision. Although he cannot tell them *exactly* when it will happen, 'I tell you this,' he says. 'The present generation will live to see it all.' Nor is this the only place the imminence of the event is stressed. In Mark again, at the beginning of Chapter 9, he says: 'I tell you this: there are some of those standing here who will not taste death before they have seen the kingdom of God already come in power.' The other Gospels have similar passages.

These clear prophecies, that the end of all things was nigh, delayed the writing of the Gospels,[4] as mentioned in Chapter 8. The steady procession of uneventful days disappointed the Church, and the death of the apostles made matters worse. In Peter's second letter he says men will ask: 'Where now is the promise of his coming? Our fathers have been laid to their rest, but still everything continues exactly as it has always been since the world began.'[5]

Jesus could not hear the clear words of God – he was a man, subject to all the restrictions of men – and as a channel of communication he was inspired but not perfect. This, his major prophecy, was not fulfilled.

The other main predictions were concerned with his death. On three occasions[6] he told the disciples what would happen to him, including his being condemned to death by the chief priests and officials and his recovery from death three days afterwards. In other places he reinforces this idea of recovery after three days, the most memorable being in Matthew (12:39-40), where he says: 'It is a wicked, godless generation that asks for a sign; and the only sign that will be given it is the sign of the prophet Jonah. Jonah was in the sea-monster's belly for three days and three nights, and in the same way the Son of Man will be three days and three nights in the bowels of the earth.' Remember also the crucial claim, quoted at his trial, about rebuilding the temple in three days. This was either another prophecy, or, more likely, the same one in a different form.

Seeking inspiration through prayer was clearly a factor in such prophecies; another was study of the Scriptures, in which the word of God, channelled through previous prophets, was preserved. Jesus had a deep knowledge of the Scriptures, although there were two occasions when he either made a mistake with regard to them or his words were incorrectly recorded.[7] His study of the Scriptures led him to a conclusion on the nature of his fate. This in turn depended on the nature of the role he felt he was called upon to play.

Throughout the Gospels there is only one occasion when Jesus claims without reservation to be the Messiah, and the Gospel recording it – John – is the least reliable as far as the teaching is concerned. Furthermore, the person to whom the claim is made is – of all unlikely people – the Samaritan woman.

Since the Gospels were written when the very basis of the Church's faith was that Jesus had fulfilled the role of Messiah, this is extraordinary. Even when Jesus is asked the direct question by the High Priest, 'Are you the Messiah?' the answer is not an unqualified 'Yes', but rather 'You have said so.' And when Peter bursts out 'You are the Messiah', in Mark (8:29) and Luke (9:20), the oldest traditions,[8] Jesus does not tell Peter he is correct but silences him.

Again, it can only have been in the cause of truth that these incidents were recorded in this way. It is probable, therefore, that Jesus never made the claim, which may have been because he did not see himself as filling the role of Messiah, at least until after he offered himself up to death. One way or the other, he felt that he was singled out for a special purpose, and studied the Scriptures to see what that purpose would be.

His statements to his disciples make his conclusions clear. He was to be *Ebed Yahweh*, the Suffering Servant.[9] Through his vicarious suffering the sins of the race would be redeemed. The main text foretelling this role is in Isaiah 53, but from Jesus's words and actions it is clear that he also believed that parts of the Psalms, especially 22 and 69, were probably root sources. The rulers would take counsel against him.[10]. He would be led like a sheep to the slaughter,[11] and crucified,[12] although no bone would be broken.[13] The only relevant prediction to mention death is in Isaiah 53, and this implies recovery from it immediately afterwards:[14] the others prophesy that he will not know corruption. But of one point he could be confident. If his trust in God were such that he would die to bridge the gap between God and His Chosen Race, he could not be 'accursed of God'. He would not therefore die on the Cross.

On the evidence of the Gospels, it is highly likely that Jesus expected to be crucified, but that after three days and nights God would recognize him as the Messiah.[15] What form that recognition would take he could not know, but it would coincide with his second coming, which would bring in the Kingdom of Heaven.

From the stains on the Shroud and the written accounts, a picture of what happened can be drawn. Such was Jesus's confidence in his predictions and his God, he underwent scourging, buffeting, humiliation and mockery, and the agony of being nailed by the hands and feet. Greater love hath no man. After about three hours on the Cross, the doubt came. He knew he did not have the physical reserves to last three days and three nights, and there was no sign of any relief. In that awful moment his faith wavered. Suppose his interpretation had been wrong! Suppose he was really going to die, and be 'accursed of God'! From that infinite depth of despair came his cry, 'My God! My God! Why hast thou forsaken me?' Seeing his state, one of his soldiers offered him a sponge soaked with vinegar or wine. It went down the wrong way, and after an agonizing spell of coughing and spluttering, he collapsed to the side, falling into a coma.

From this he recovered, as the evidence of the Shroud and the New Testament shows. What experience he had in the meantime, it is impossible to tell. People who die clinically and subsequently recover tell of remarkable experiences.[16]

Who knows what the spirit of Jesus encountered while his body lay in the tomb? It is possible that he then had a confirmation that he was the promised Messiah, and that this certainty, as well as the realization that he had overcome death, was passed on to his disciples when he gathered them to him in Galilee.

It must be emphasized that this is all speculation; but with the background of the written evidence matching it so well, it makes Jesus a more credible figure, and a more inspiring example, than the strange God-and-man combination of traditional Christian dogma.

This personalizing of Jesus also adds substance to the roles of others connected with him, particularly Caiaphas and Judas Iscariot.

Consider how Jesus must have appeared to Caiaphas. He was apparently claiming to be the Messiah, or at least so the crowds believed. If he really was the Messiah, Caiaphas and the Temple should have acknowledged his authority. But could he be? How could the Messiah be a Galilean, and the son of a carpenter? More than this, he consorted with disreputable people, ignored the Sabbath observance and other laws. God's Anointed could not possibly behave in this way. And yet how could one be sure that he was *not* the Messiah?

Caiaphas took the wisest course. Because Jesus drew large crowds he was a threat to the peace, and if things got out of hand the Romans would suppress the trouble with their usual efficiency. It was clearly good political sense that one man should die so that the race should be saved. But in addition it was good religious sense, for it tested the man's claim. If he really was the Messiah, God would not allow him to die on the Cross. It was trial by ordeal. According to Matthew (27: 41-43), the chief priests, lawyers and elders even went to the place of execution to see the outcome for themselves. 'Let him come down from the cross,' they said, 'and then we will believe him. Did he trust in God? Let God rescue him, if he wants him – for he said he was God's son.' When he remained suspended in agony their suspicion that his claims were false hardened into conviction and their mockery of the victim increased. When Caiaphas heard that Jesus had certainly died he must have felt very satisfied with the action he had taken.

Caiaphas is pictured in the Gospels as a devilish advocate, responsible for condemning the Son of God to death. Yet he was a man, as Jesus was a man, and if his motives are analysed his actions seem reasonable. The political ends – then as now – justified the means.

The other figure who now needs reassessing in the light of this role of Jesus is Judas, and the same light can give roundness and reality to the normal black silhouette. How *could* any man be a disciple of one such as Jesus for at least two years and then betray him for a relatively small sum of money? It makes no sense.

Once again the layers of interpretation have to be stripped off the relevant accounts. This means dealing, not only with the evangelists, but also with the translators. They, too, were interpreting the texts with this dark image of a wicked man before them, and this must have affected their choice of words.

The key Greek word in this context is *paradidomi* and its derivatives. In the Concordance of the Greek New Testament there are 121 entries for this word, which is translated in many ways, most as 'handed over', 'entrusted', 'given up', 'commended' and 'consigned'. Now these are relatively innocuous phrases, and if Judas's act of handing over Jesus to the authorities was commonly expressed in this way, he might be thought of more sympathetically. However, of the 34 times when Judas is the subject of the verb or the noun associated with this word, in 31 cases the translation is 'betray' or 'traitor'; in the remaining three instances the translation is 'put into their power', 'handed over' and 'brought to his death'. There are 87 cases where *paradidomi* is used with other subjects than Judas, and in only four cases, Matthew 10:21 and 24:10, Mark 13:12 and Luke 21:16, is the word 'betray' used; three of those four refer to the same words of Jesus, in his prophecy of the end of all things. This seems manifestly unfair to Judas. Perhaps 'handed over', assuming he had the consent of Jesus, would be a fairer description.

The written evidence suggests that Jesus expected to be

arrested by the authorities when he entered Jerusalem. Not only this, he seemed to want it to happen in order to fulfil the role suggested by his reading of the Scriptures. He was to be the Suffering Servant of Isaiah 53, the scapegoat for the sins of Israel, offering himself as Isaac was offered for sacrifice by Abraham, and trusting to be saved from death at the last moment, as Isaac was.

The Temple police tried to arrest him, as he would have wished, but the crowd prevented them. During the day the authorities could not apprehend him, so Jesus needed a go-between. As I have pointed out elsewhere,[17] Judas was the obvious disciple to pick. He was the one Judean, so by language, looks, education and contacts, he was the most suitable.

It could have been by agreement, therefore, that Judas arranged for Jesus to be 'handed over', and when that interpretation is applied to the written accounts, little points of agreement can be seen behind the veneer added by the evangelists with the developed view of later years. At the preliminary meeting between Judas and the chief priests,[18] the meeting-place of the Garden of Gethsemane could have been suggested. At the Last Supper, Jesus announced that one of the disciples was going to hand him over to the authorities, and this alarmed the others who were not privy to the plan.

> One of them, the disciple he loved, was reclining close beside Jesus. So Simon Peter nodded to him and said, 'Ask him who it is he means.' That disciple, as he reclined, leaned back close to Jesus and asked, 'Lord, who is it?' Jesus replied, 'It is the man to whom I give this piece of bread when I have dipped it in the dish.' Then, after dipping it in the dish, he took it out and gave it to Judas son of Simon Iscariot . . . Jesus said to him, 'Do quickly what you have to do.' No one at the table understood what he meant by this [John 13: 23-28].

Judas left, as arranged. However, it would seem that the assembly of the arresting party by Caiaphas took longer than anticipated, perhaps because Pilate had insisted on the presence of some Roman troops. This would explain why

Jesus spent so long in the Garden of Gethsemane. His disciples, who kept falling asleep, must have wondered why they could not leave and go to their beds. When Judas finally appeared with the party Jesus kissed him. 'Friend,' he said, 'do what you are here to do.' (Matthew 26: 50)

So Jesus was probably handed over, with his consent, and not betrayed. Judas, too, would have expected him to receive Messianic recognition on the Cross, after three days and three nights, as he had foretold. It would thus have been a terrible shock, that Friday afternoon, when eye-witnesses entered the city with the news that Jesus had died. They had seen his chest pierced! There could be no doubt.

What Judas would have felt then!

No wonder he killed himself.

References

1. Mark 1: 34.
2. Robinson, J. A. T., *The Human Face of God,* S.C.M., 1973, pp. 97-98.
3. Vermes, G., *Jesus the Jew,* Fontana/Collins, 1976, Chapter 4.
4. Grant, F. C., *The Gospels – Their Origin and Growth,* Faber and Faber, 1965, pp. 29, 33.
5. II Peter 3; 4.
6. In Mark see 8: 31, 9:31 and 10: 33-34, and there are parallel texts.
7. Mark 2: 26 and Matthew 23: 35. See Brown, R. E., *Jesus, God and Man,* Chapman, 1967, pp. 51-54.
8. Brown, R. E., op. cit., p. 82.
9. Cullmann, O., *The Christology of the New Testament,* S.C.M., 1963, pp. 61-69.
10. Psalm 22:2, and Psalm 41: 5 and 7.
11. Isaiah 53: 7.
12. Psalm 22: 16.
13. Psalm 22: 17.
14. Isaiah 53: 9-10.
15. Hoare, R. P., *The Testimony of the Shroud,* Quartet, 1978, Chapter 10.
16. Ritchie, G., *Return from Tomorrow,* Kingsway, 1978. Also Moody, R. A., *Life after Life,* Bantam Books, 1976.
17. Hoare, R. P., op. cit., pp. 103-109.
18. Mark 14: 10-11.

Fourteen
IMPOSING PROBABILITIES

To prove beyond *all* doubt that the Shroud is genuine, and that the body which left the stains was that of Jesus, is impossible. However strong a case is made, multitudes will refuse to believe it. Part of the trouble is that objectivity is displaced as soon as any element of faith enters into the argument.

Because of this, the first part of the book tried to avoid any mention of religion, in the hope that an unprejudiced assessment could be made of the evidence presented by the cloth. However, there is no doubt that many readers, knowing the identity of the person whose body apparently produced the stains on the burial-cloth, will have seen the directions some of the conclusions to Part One were taking and refused to accept them.

In the second part of the book this danger could no longer be avoided. Every reader's life, whatever his beliefs, must have been affected to a very great extent by Jesus Christ, so that judgement is bound to be coloured by involvement. It is thus difficult to study the argument purely on its merits. There has been a clear precedent for this.

On 21 April 1902, the results of Vignon's research on the Shroud were given to the illustrious French Academy of Sciences by Yves Delage. After describing the visible and experimental evidence, he deduced that the stains could not have been painted but they must have been produced by 'a physico-chemical phenomenon'. He then went on to compare the details of the stains with the written evidence of the Gospels, and came to the conclusion that 'the man on the Shroud was the Christ'.[1] Yves Delage was well known for his agnostic views.

The Secretary of the Academy refused to print any part of the paper that asserted the image was of Jesus, and a secret committee rejected Delage's request that the Academy ask for a more complete investigation of the relic. Vignon's work had been done using photographs. Outside the Academy the reception was equally surprising to Delage, most critics reacting hysterically, and Delage himself was the subject of savage abuse. In a letter to the *Revue Scientifique* he wrote:

> I willingly recognize that none of these arguments offers the features of an irrefutable demonstration; but it must be recognized that their sum constitutes a bundle of imposing probabilities, some of which are very close to being proven . . . A religious question has been needlessly injected into a problem which in itself is purely scientific, with the result that feelings have run high, and reason has been led astray. If, instead of Christ, there were a question of some person like a Sargon, an Achilles or one of the pharaohs, no one would have thought of making any objections . . . I have been faithful to the true spirit of Science in treating this question, intent only on the truth, not concerned in the least whether it would affect the interests of any religious party . . . I recognize Christ as a historical personage and I see no reason why anyone should be scandalized that there still exist material traces of his earthly life.[2]

Bearing in mind that nothing has been proved for certain, and that the best that can be hoped for are probabilities so imposing that they compel trust, it is worth summarizing what this study of the cloth and the written evidence has shown.

1. The cloth known as the Turin Shroud is genuine, and the marks on it of the front and back of a human body were formed naturally from a real body.

2. That body belonged to the historical character known as Jesus Christ.

3. The marks show that he was scourged, and then crucified by being nailed to the normal sort of *crux immissa* with a *sedile* on which he could sit.

4. After a considerable time upright on the *sedile,* he slipped unconscious to the right and hung in that position for a similar period.

5. His legs were not broken, which is recorded as the normal way of despatching victims, but he was stabbed in the right side of the chest. This would have confirmed that he was dead by the standards of the time.

6. His body was placed in the Shroud, unwashed and unanointed, in a trough-like space such as was usual in a first-century Jewish tomb. His head was pillowed below the Shroud, and there was another pile of material stuffed below his feet.

7. Since decomposition did not set in to spoil the image on the cloth, the body must have left the cloth in less than about thirty-six hours.

So far the Shroud can be taken as material evidence that Jesus Christ lived, was scourged and crucified, died absolutely by the standards of the time, and left the tomb empty, exactly as described in the Gospels. As a record of these events the Shroud becomes the First Gospel, the pre-eminent witness, being both contemporary and independent of the faults of human witnesses and oral transmission.

Although Christians firmly declare that their faith in no way depends on material evidence like the Shroud, and thus it follows that its authenticity makes no difference to them, confirmation of this sort must surely help to strengthen their faith.

8. There is remarkable corroboration between the stains on the Shroud and two of the 'Beloved Disciple'

sections of John's Gospel. They describe the bowing of the head, the wound in the chest, the blood and water spurting out, the legs being left unbroken and the two separate bundles of material in the tomb, none of which are mentioned in the Synoptics. This shows them to be genuine eye-witness fragments of the greatest possible historical value.

That again should confirm Christian belief, for biblical scholars have sometimes dismissed John's Gospel as being totally untrustworthy historically. Indeed, one historian at least feels that 'from the historical viewpoint, the Church committed an error when it declared the Gospel to be orthodox'.[3]

But some of the further conclusions are more difficult for those of rigid beliefs to accept.

9. The body of Jesus, while dead by the standards of the time, was in what is now recognized as a deep coma, from which a body may die or recover consciousness.

10. The body and the Shroud were removed from the tomb during the Saturday night.

11. In view of the written records that Jesus was physically alive after the tomb was found empty, he must have recovered consciousness. He would have needed tending for no more than two or three weeks at the most, and could then have gone to search for his scattered disciples. The 'seven-week gap', between Resurrection shortly after Crucifixion and the announcement by the joyful disciples in Jerusalem that Jesus had risen from the dead, is more understandable in view of the recovery time.

Having determined the sequence of events that could have produced the markings on the Shroud and the written accounts, the people concerned in the narrative were examined. What were their motives in doing what they did? What do their actions reveal about their characters?

Here the material evidence of the Shroud was left behind, and attention was focused on the less reliable written sources. Logical deduction merged into speculation, the scientist's method into the historian's. If a rational explanation of the material evidence can be found, can it fit the historical evidence?

Considering the removal of the body from the tomb and the need to nurse it to full recovery, there is at least one perfectly reasonable solution. Joseph of Arimathea and probably Nicodemus (who appears only in John's Gospel) are likely to have been responsible for both. They took to the tomb at least some of the materials necessary for a proper burial, but because of the onset of the Sabbath they could give the body only a temporary covering. They would almost certainly have returned to the tomb after the Sabbath was over, at sunset on Saturday, to complete the proper rites. Finding the body in an unnatural state – now known as a coma – they decided against leaving it in an unguarded tomb and took it away, with the Shroud for warmth, to watch developments. In view of the very wide social divisions of the time, it is no surprise that the disciples never discovered their actions.

Working back from the Gentile through the early Jewish Church, from Pauline and Johannine theology through the Gospels and back to the original sermon of Peter, the character of Jesus had its outer layers of divinity stripped off to reveal a whole, Jewish man, but a man singled out by God. It is likely that he was a first-century Jew who believed he had a commission from God to his fellow Jews, that he interpreted his role as the bearer of his nation's sins who would redeem them with their God by sacrificing his own life. While not claiming to be the Messiah during his life, he believed that if he offered himself up to crucifixion, he would be saved from death at the last moment, to return as the Messiah of his nation.

Judas's motives for handing over Jesus to the authorities become clearer in the light of this interpretation, for if Jesus shared this conception of his fate with Judas, he would have chosen him to arrange for the authorities to take him into custody without danger to the other disciples. This gives

Judas a credible motive for his action, and agrees with details in the Gospel stories. The description there, that a devil suddenly entered into someone who had apparently been a good disciple up to that moment, is more difficult to believe.

Showing that the Resurrection was not supernatural, in that a physical body recovered from a deep coma, means that what happened to that body finally is now a matter for speculation. The Shroud cannot help there, nor the Gospel accounts. The Ascension is described in the doubtful, extended Mark, in Luke and in Acts 1: 9-10. The Luke and Acts accounts, although by the same author, differ considerably.

It is true Jesus still had a real, live body, a body that people could see and feel, and that needed to eat and drink. It follows that this body would have had to die finally. No evidence survives where or when that happened. But does that matter? Perhaps, soon after leaving his disciples, he died somewhere in Palestine, and his bones may lie there still. But bones are useless without flesh and blood, and the whole body is of no consequence unless invigorated and controlled by the spirit within.

The deduction that the Resurrection can be explained rationally, and that God did not step outside the physical laws of the Universe to translate the body of Jesus from substance to a uniquely observable spirit, may disturb some Christians whose faith depends on a supernatural explanation. On the other hand, in this materialistic age very many people are repelled by the traditional teaching of the Church on the events of the first Easter. The Resurrection is so alien to their experience of the physical environment that they regard it as myth, which then develops into a doubt that Jesus even existed. For them the Shroud may be crucial, for it is material evidence that Jesus lived, died, and rose again without breaking the laws of science.

While explaining how the Resurrection could have occurred naturally, we are dealing only with the material plane. The whole story of the Shroud is so remarkable – from the formation of the image, its perfection, the qualities of the cloth, the timing and conditions of the Crucifixion and entombment, right down to the 1532 fire damage and the preservation of the Shroud through the centuries – that many will see in it the signs of divine guidance. The material side is only one half of the story. The other is even more important.

This suggests another question. If the Shroud has been preserved in this remarkable way, does this imply a purpose? Only in the twentieth century, with the tools of modern science, is there a chance that the Shroud can be finally deciphered. There *must* be a message in it for us.

If these conclusions are correct, there may be a need to alter certain current Christian beliefs. The Shroud shows how the Resurrection was physically possible. It wrapped a real man rather than a god. That man, if Jesus, was a very special person, however, although how special is a matter of personal belief. In terms of physical energy, the laws of the material universe are hardly bent by the belief in a special creation at the moment of conception resulting in the Virgin birth. However, if Jesus was a pure man rather than God-as-man, the concept of the Trinity may need amending to bring it closer to the belief in God of the original Jerusalem Church. Could that be a purpose of the Shroud? The Church would still retain in the historical Jesus a man so transparent to the power and message of God that he would be the perfect example for all of us and the channel through whose words the will of God can be most easily determined.

Religion should develop; it is the inflexibility of creeds that causes conflict. Sects tend to fight over differences rather than rejoice in agreements. If only the Shroud could be accepted as genuine material evidence, and the message it bears analyzed and accepted, Christians might approach unity. If Jews were also to accept its message, they might find in its stains the conviction that Jesus did not die on the Cross, was not 'accursed of God', and in fact did receive the Messianic recognition. Lastly, the division with the Muslim world could also be healed, for Muslims already recognize Jesus as a prophet of God, but cannot accept that he died on the Cross or was divine while on earth.

This is all too much to hope for, no doubt; but there may be great benefits from analyzing the message borne by the Shroud. The first step must be verifying its age by carbon dating. While the Church has refused this test, scientists have been hesitant to devote themselves to the study of the relic, for there is the constant suspicion that its guardians must have something to hide. Material has been cut off, and more can be removed from behind the patches, to provide samples for hundreds of tests. There is no need to wait until the accuracy is to within a few years over 2,000. The argument at the moment is whether the stains were formed by painting in the fourteenth century or naturally in the first.

The method has been accurate enough to sort that out for years. Can it be that the Church is afraid of finding out the truth?

References

1. Walsh, J., *The Shroud,* Star Book, W. H. Allen, 1979, pp. 75-76.
2. Humber, T., *The Fifth Gospel,* Pocket Book, 1974, pp. 109-111.
3. Kasemann, E., *The Testament of Jesus,* S.C.M., 1968, p. 176.

SELECT
BIBLIOGRAPHY

Apart from the papers in scientific journals, Bible dictionaries and other reference books, the following works are quoted or referred to in the text.

Pierre, Barbet, *A Doctor at Cavalry,* Image books, N.Y. (1963).
S. G. F. Brandon, *The Fall of Jerusalem and the Christian Church,* S.P.C.K. (1951).
S. G. F. Brandon, *The Trial of Jesus of Nazareth,* Batsford (1968).
Raymond E. Brown, *Jesus, God and Man,* Chapman (1967).
Werner Bulst, *The Shroud of Turin,* Bruce Publishing Co., Milwaukee (1957).
Oscar Cullmann, *The Christology of the New Testament,* S.C.M. (1963).
Don Cupitt and Peter Armstrong, *Who was Jesus?,* B.B.C. (1977).
Daniel-Rops, *Jesus in His Time,* Eyre and Spottiswoode (1955).
Charles Harold Dodds, *The Founder of Christianity,* Collins (1972).
Floyd V. Filson, *A New Testament History,* S.C.M. (1965).
Birger Gerhardsson, *The Origins of the Gospel Traditions,* S.C.M. (1979).
Frederick Clifton Grant, *The Gospels – Their Origin and Growth,* Faber and Faber (1965).
Harold Alfred Guy, *The Study of the Gospels,* Macmillan (1967).
Martin Hengel, *Crucifixion,* S.C.M. (1977).
Rodney Hoare, *The Testimony of the Shroud,* Quartet Books (1978).
Thomas Humber, *The Fifth Gospel,* Pocket Books, N.Y. (1974).

R. W. Hynek, *The True Likeness,* Sheed and Ward, N.Y. (1951).

M. R. James, *The Apocryphal New Testament,* Oxford University Press (1924).

Peter Jennings (ed.), *Face to Face with the Turin Shroud,* Mayhew-McCrimmon (1978).

Ernst Kasemann, *The Testament of Jesus,* S.C.M. (1968).

Xavier Leon-Dufour, *The Gospels and the Jesus of History,* Collins (1968).

Bruce Metzger, *The New Testament, its Background, Growth and Content,* Lutterworth Press (1969).

Charles Leslie Mitton, *Jesus: the Fact behind the Faith,* Mowbray (1975).

Raymond A. Moody, *Life after Life,* Bantam Books (1976).

Frank Morison, *Who Moved the Stone?,* Faber and Faber (1930).

Alfred O'Rahilly, *The Burial of Christ,* Cork University Press (1942).

Gerald Priestland, *Yours Faithfully,* Collins (1979).

Peter M. Rinaldi, *The Man in the Shroud,* Futura (1974).

George Ritchie, *Return from Tomorrow,* Kingsway Press (1978).

John A. T. Robinson, *The Human Face of God,* S.C.M. (1973).

H. David Sox, *File on the Shroud,* Coronet Books (1978).

H. David Sox, *The Image on the Shroud,* Unwin Paperbacks (1981).

K. E. Stevenson and G. R. Habermas, *Verdict on the Shroud,* Robert Hale (1982).

Geza Vermes, *Jesus the Jew,* Fontana (1976).

Paul Vignon, *The Shroud of Christ,* Constable (1902).

John Walsh, *The Shroud,* W. H. Allen (1979).

Robert K. Wilcox, *Shroud,* Corgi Books (1978).

Ian Wilson, *The Turin Shroud,* Gollancz (1978).

INDEX